Cahokia's Complexities

Archaeology of the American South:
New Directions and Perspectives

A Dan Josselyn Memorial Fund Publication

Cahokia's Complexities

Ceremonies and Politics of the First Mississippian Farmers

SUSAN M. ALT

THE UNIVERSITY OF ALABAMA PRESS
Tuscaloosa

The University of Alabama Press
Tuscaloosa, Alabama 35487-0380
uapress.ua.edu

Typeface: Bembo and Eurostile

Cover image: Grossmann site celt cache; courtesy of Susan M. Alt
Cover design: Michele Myatt Quinn

Library of Congress Cataloging-in-Publication Data

Names: Alt, Susan M., 1959– author.
Title: Cahokia's complexities : ceremonies and politics of the first Mississippian farmers / Susan M. Alt.
Description: Tuscaloosa : The University of Alabama Press, 2018. | Series: Archaeology of the American south: new directions and perspectives | Includes bibliographical references and index.
Identifiers: LCCN 2017038248| ISBN 9780817319762 (cloth : alk. paper) | ISBN 9780817391737 (e-book)
Subjects: LCSH: Mississippian culture—Illinois—American Bottom. | Cahokia Mounds State Historic Park (Ill.)—Antiquities. | Social archaeology—Illinois—American Bottom. | Indians of North America—Illinois—American Bottom—Antiquities.
Classification: LCC E99.M6815 A48 2018 | DDC 299.7—dc23
LC record available at https://lccn.loc.gov/2017038248

For Frances Fasano Alt, who became my mom, and taught me to always keep learning and trying to do and be better.

Contents

Illustrations

Figures

Tables

Acknowledgments

The excavation of the Grossmann site, which is detailed in this book, was possible only because of Tim Pauketat, his vision and his Richland Archaeological Project, and his funding from National Science Foundation Grant BCS-0219308 and National Geographic Society Grant 7313–02. Cahokia mounds grants helped with dates and digitizing. A National Science Foundation fellowship made my fieldwork, analysis, and write-up of such a large project possible. But none of this work could have happened without the earliest research at the site by the Illinois State Archaeological Survey and its willingness to share its data and expertise. Tom Emerson, in particular, whose work this book builds on, has been an inspiration and a mentor. I also thank Doug Jackson for his kindness in sharing his wisdom and experience about all things Mississippian. Connie Stohlmann and the TRDS land company were kind enough to permit and facilitate work on the site property.

Grossmann is unusual because an entire village was excavated. But that never would have been possible but for the extraordinary group of people who chose to work and do their field school at this site. I have never worked with people so thoroughly dedicated to the work at hand, and who made working together so much fun. I can't imagine field seasons as intense or with a better group of people ever again—I will always miss those years! Jeff Kruchten, Mike Litchford, Steph Glienke, Tracey Steffgen, Tamira Brennan, Holley Gonzales, Phil Millhouse, Ian Fricker, and Cari Baxter were crew and field supervisors extraordinaire. I can't thank them enough, and I am proud to have worked with them. The field school students also deserve thanks for all their hard work and for excelling under grueling conditions. It is exciting to know where you are today, and to think that Grossmann might have had something to do with your careers!

I appreciate even more now the importance of a strong woman as mentor and role model, and Olga Soffer was the no-nonsense inspiration that I needed. Her example, support, and advice got me through the initial drafts of this book. The final draft might never have come together without the support and encouragement of my husband, Tim Pauketat. I thank Meghan Howey and an anonymous reviewer who provided feedback and suggestions that have helped strengthen this book. I also thank everyone from the press for all their hard work in helping improve this book and bring it to completion. Any and all errors are my own.

Introduction

Structure of the Book

This book presents data from the Grossmann site (11S1131), a Cahokian settlement that was excavated in its entirety. I will argue that Grossmann was a Cahokian administrative center where processes such as hybridity intertwined with ritual and politics. After reviewing some useful concepts—including complexity, hybridity, memory, and thirdspace—in the first chapter, I examine the Cahokia case in broad strokes in Chapter 2. I compare details of the cultural landscape in the floodplain around Cahokia proper before turning, in Chapter 3, to the farming villages of the Richland uplands east of the floodplain. In Chapter 4, I focus on the layout and architecture of one extraordinary upland site, Grossmann, 16 km southeast of Cahokia. Because of its architectural forms and material remains, I identify Grossmann as a minor-administrative or Cahokian ritual-residential outlier, likely one of several such places in that agricultural district where local farmers might have seen or in some way participated in Cahokian ritual and ceremony.

In doing so, I follow Thomas Emerson (1997a, 1997c) in identifying a kind of "nodal" settlement in the American Bottom region, a place where rural, dispersed people had their needs administered by Cahokia. Cahokian authority, Emerson originally suggested, was emplaced in the countryside via distinctive architectural forms and ceremonial practices. This effectively "ruralized" the farming population there, to adopt the words of Norman Yoffee (2005).

How this happened is apparent in the materiality of the Grossmann site, as presented in Chapters 4 and 5. Because of the totality of evidence from Grossmann, where the entire settlement was excavated in three field seasons, I argue that Cahokians managed or ministered to the needs of upland farmers through the materiality of the place and its assemblages of things. In fact, as concluded in Chapter 6, the upland settlements clarify the history of greater Cahokia. That is, not only is it likely that Cahokians founded a series of "nodal" administrative centers to more fully integrate rural people into the Cahokian sphere, it appears that temple renewal events, first-fruit ceremonies, and the mediating treatment of the dead here—especially as it happened through a series of key events and objects in the context of on-site rituals—entangled politics and religion and enabled Cahokian "control" of the farming hinterlands but also brought about the beginning of the end of Cahokia.

Grossmann and the upland sites east of Cahokia also help us to decenter politics by recognizing that the political realm was inseparable from farmers and nonhuman powers. Grossmann was, in essence, a "thirdspace" that facilitated the creation of new cultural forms (Bhabha 1994; Soja 1996). As such, it provides insights into how any society might expand and contract in a short period of time. Here, we might see how upland people and their things and practices were folded into a Cahokian sphere to create a novel kind of complexity, one comprising a web of ancestors, powers, and places.

1
Cahokia's Complex Relationships

All forms of culture are continually in a process of hybridity.
—Homi K. Bhabha, "The Third Space"

The reasons that early cities and ceremonial centers rose and fell in the distant past have been sought for centuries. How did this happen? Why did it happen? And how was it related to identity and identity politics? Such questions can be asked of Cahokia, the great pre-Columbian monumental complex and population center in the middle of North America, in part because of the rich archaeological information at our fingertips (Figure 1.1).

We know that Cahokia was the first, and exponentially the largest, of the "Mississippian" centers that appeared across midwestern and southeastern North America after A.D. 1000 (Blitz 2010). Located in the American Bottom region of southwestern Illinois, the central complex of Cahokia covered more than 12 km^2 and contained more than 120 earthen mounds, several carefully engineered plazas, and thousands of pole-and-thatch buildings. Recent work at and around this ancient core has documented other "precincts" and diverse sorts of outliers and "shrine complexes" (Alt 2012; Alt and Pauketat 2017; Pauketat and Alt 2015; Pauketat et al. 2015). Yet despite the rich archaeological record at and around Cahokia, it defies simple explanation, possibly because our explanatory constructs have remained oversimplistic. Single causal factors are still too often sought rather than complex histories (Alt 2010).

Hence, my goal with this book is twofold. First, I make the case for Cahokian administration of the upland farmlands east of the city. Cahokians and Mississippian immigrant farmers were in direct contact out in the rural landscape. What were the effects? That leads to my second goal: I demonstrate how such administration, in the context of the immigra-

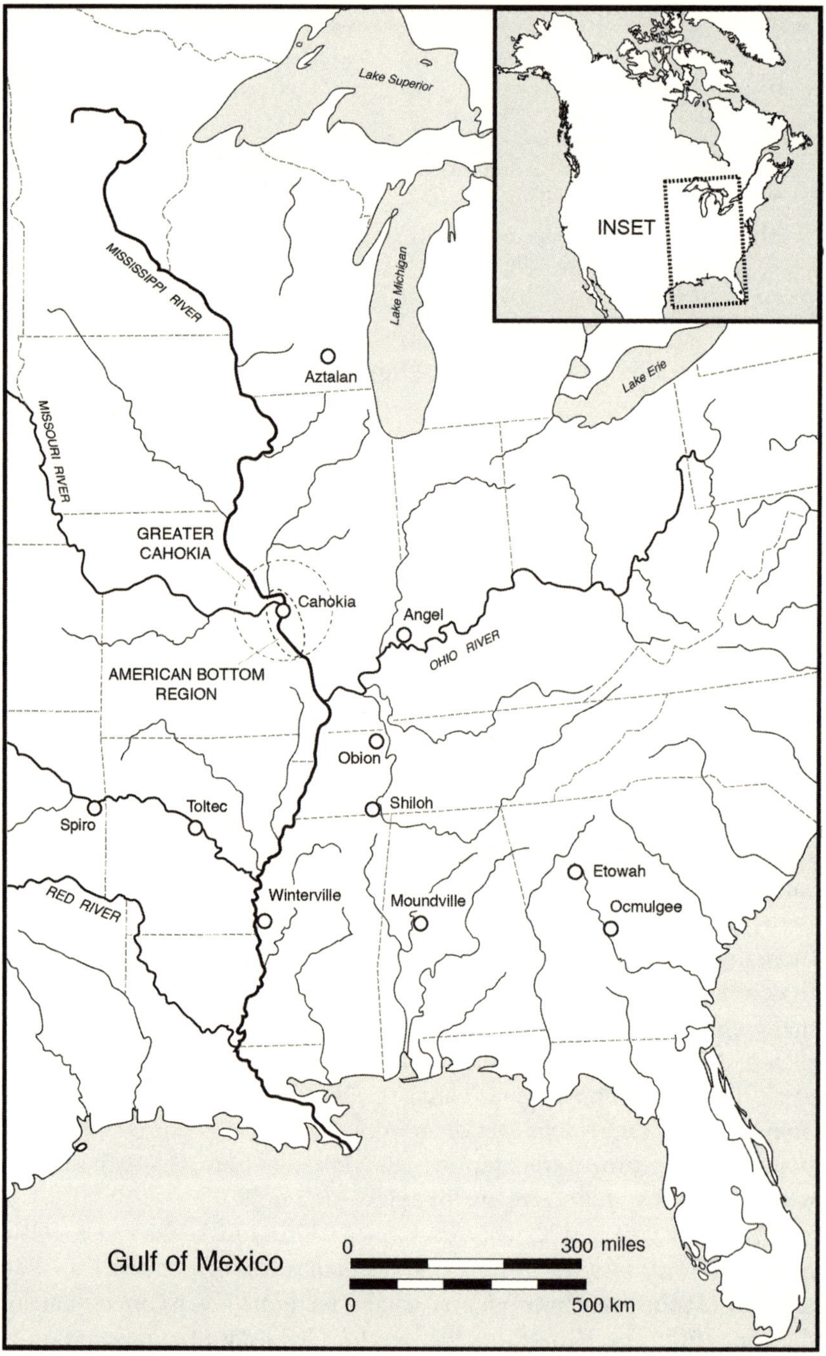

Figure 1.1. Location of Cahokia in North America.

tion and resettlement hypothesized for the early phases of Cahokia, generated a novel kind of early Mississippian culture.

In this, I adapt the concept of "hybridity" more familiar to studies of cultural contacts and historic eras (Bhabha 1994). I use the term as a heuristic alongside other, more familiar concepts (practice, memory, power), focusing primarily on the creation of "thirdspaces"—those locations or contexts where differences meet and innovations occur. There are limitations to the concept of hybridity as implemented in historic archaeology (Liebmann 2013, 2015; Silliman 2013, 2015; van Dommelen 1997), but it also has unrealized benefits when applied to our thinking about Mississippian social change. For instance, it is one of a suite of concepts that historicize the past by acknowledging that all people played a part in what came to be. In addition, concepts such as hybridity and thirdspace dovetail with recent relational approaches to things, object agency, and affects, empowering material culture and space to play an active role in the shaping of human history (see, for example, Alberti et al. 2011; Gosden 2005; Tarlow 2012; Witmore 2014), in the present case the construction of "Mississippian culture" at and around Cahokia.

Homi Bhabha (1994) originally suggested that when people with different traditions, habits, and expectations meet, a space outside the normal rules of engagement opens up that permits new social relations to materialize. This place of engagement-with-difference permits, if not requires, new social memories, cultural practices, and cultural landscapes to develop. It also suggests that complexity could not have emerged and emanated from single sources—say, political centers—but must have been continually produced at a series of sites throughout a region, as people, along with their things and places, enacted or commemorated their identities daily (Van Dyke and Alcock 2003). In the end, I suggest that we need to extend such a concept as hybridity to the engagements between human persons and places, objects, and other-than-human persons.

Understanding what people did and why they did it is impossible without thinking about their places and things more broadly (Alberti et al. 2011; Harvey 2006; Jones and Alberti 2013; Witmore 2014). This makes population or ceremonial "centers" considerably more complex historically than many archaeologists might acknowledge. That is, complexity, strictly defined, is more than political and even more than human. This flies in the face of many "Mississippian" period studies in the Midwest and Southeast, which have adhered to the dictum that the simplest explanations are the best (Muller 1997).

I disagree with the implications of that approach, as I explain below, in large part because it forces us to reject complexity before our investigations even begin (Alt, ed. 2010). Indeed, I have concluded that the old question of complexity—were Mississippian societies complex?—is unproductive. Building from the notion of hybridity, I instead consider "*how* were Mississippian relationships complex?" (Nelson 1995). To ask how is to encourage researchers to seek the social, religious, and political processes whereby complexity was created. Those processes for me entail untangling the relationships among all people, places, and things, especially as evident in the remains of extraordinary collective happenings. Such group events allow me to focus on the process of hybridity.

The evidence suggests that Cahokia, and Mississippian complexity in general, was generated in such ways. This generation, especially as it involved the alteration of the central Mississippi valley's social landscape in the middle of the eleventh century A.D., has been called the Mississippian world's "Big Bang," the moment(s) when Cahokia was transformed from an ungainly Late Woodland village into a Mississippian city (Pauketat 1997). Previously, I have argued that this Cahokian moment was inextricably tied to the arrival of immigrants from local and more distant Native American towns in the American Bottom, which is the wide floodplain around the Cahokia site that is at the heart of the "greater Cahokia" region (Alt 2001, 2002a, 2006a). The presence of these immigrants, especially in the numbers now apparent, had a profound effect in the Mississippi valley (Slater et al. 2014). That is, the mixing of local and nonlocal people at and around Cahokia would have necessitated large-scale negotiations of difference in people's ways of being in and relating to the world. Cahokia, in short, was a fertile ground in which the creation of new cultural forms might happen. The uplands east of Cahokia—where Cahokian administrators met relocated Mississippian farmers—embodied this process as well.

Complexity

Complexity remains an ambiguous and yet loaded concept. Archaeologists consider societies complex when they are strongly centralized, hierarchically organized, or internally differentiated in some way (Chapman 2003; McGuire 1983; Neitzel 1999). The particular dimension of complexity under consideration seems to vary greatly, and yet complexity is often glossed as if it were a universal and constant referent.

The questions of complexity have been the subtext for much research into the Mississippian societies of the Midwest and Southeast. Most often, this begins with arguments over classification, with Mississippian societies typically branded as "chiefdoms." Mississippian towns, for many, are assumed to have been the administrative or ritual centers of such chiefdoms, some more or less complex than others. Some researchers even subdivide Mississippian chiefdoms into one or another subtype, based in part on assumptions about alternative organizational forms or histories (Anderson 1994, 1999; Beck 2003; Blitz 1999, 2010; Cobb 2003; King 2003; Knight and Steponaitis 1998; Muller 1986, 1997; Pauketat 2007; Scarry 1996; Steponaitis and Scarry 2016; Steponaitis 1983, 1991; Trubitt 2000; Welch 1991). The "archaeological procedure has been to correlate one or more central features of a favorite ethnographic type with some excavated material; then the archaeologist can extrapolate all of the rest of the characteristics of the type and so bring the not-directly-observable [*sic*] dimensions of ancient reality into view" (Yoffee 1993:60–61). This procedure remains in place for many despite widely recognized problems with the chiefdom concept and its subdivisions.

Few of these solutions to the question of Mississippian complexity—even those that subdivide categories—have produced significant new insights into the past. After all, when encumbered by taxonomy, what can we possibly end up learning beyond the attributes that supposedly accompany other examples of the type of society in question? There is simply too much variability among the societies lumped under the umbrella of the chiefdom (Feinman and Neitzel 1984).

There are other regions in the world where researchers have been bogged down in definitional disagreements over the question of complexity. While southeastern archaeologists dispute what to call Cahokia (Cobb 2003; Pauketat 2007), southwestern archaeologists have debated whether and what to label Chaco, Hohokam, and Casas Grandes (Feinman et al. 2000). Mesoamericanists get hung up on who had the first city and whether Olmec was a mother culture (Clark 2004; Flannery 1998). Mesopotamian experts still seem unable to agree on whether or how to categorize Ubaid polities or even Uruk cities (Yoffee 2005). There can be no way to solve the problem of categorization, even by identifying a single feature, say a palace or a storehouse, as a marker of some organizational threshold (Flannery 1998). Such cookbook prescriptions rely on assumptions of universal correlations between material types and human actions and beliefs.

In his detailed comparison of Chaco Canyon, La Quemada, and Paquimé, Ben Nelson (1995) suggested circumventing the categorical arguments inherent to common archaeological practices. He suggested that we ask "how were societies complex?" rather than "were they complex?" The latter question can be answered with a yes or no, while the former requires elaboration, and such elaboration better serves the advancement of anthropological knowledge (see also Neitzel 1999; Possehl 1997). In a similar attempt to avoid the hot-button terms that fuel debates in the southwestern United States, "rituality" has been used to describe Chaco Canyon as a place that was complex in nonhierarchical ways (see Yoffee et al. 1999:266). These efforts differ from the usual categorizations in that they shift focus to what was occurring in a particular place, rather than try to draw broad categories that ultimately negate the unique characteristics of individual societies. As these efforts began to suggest in the 1990s, the goal of investigations into past societies might more productively move away from cataloging traits by focusing instead on the configuration of practices and relationships in some part of the world.

Of course, to do this—to determine how people lived on a day-to-day basis as well as what people did on special occasions—one needs multiple, robust lines of evidence. And when one has those, it becomes difficult to sustain any classification of societal types. The greater Cahokia case is the best example of this reality, as we shall see, but there have been other recent shifts away from approaches that measure political-economic complexity and toward understanding how people "lived" their economies or practiced politics. In eastern North America, these tend to elevate heterarchy, communalism, and gender over hierarchy in Mississippian developments (Sullivan and Rodning 2001). Researchers at Moundville are now looking more closely at religion, ritual practice, and the hinterlands for better explanations of Moundville histories (Steponaitis and Scarry 2016). By doing so, they have begun to interrogate social histories rather than imagine oversimplistic social-evolutionary trajectories.

It is in such a historical vein that I make my examination of the complexity of particular places, practices, material assemblages, and identities. In the following sections, I open up the notion of hybridity with the help of concepts such as materiality, memory, thirdspace, and object agency. The result, I assert, turns the question of causality on its head. The hybridity of settlements and their material assemblages was not a reflection of some society's complexity but was, in effect, the cause of that so-called society. In later chapters, we will see how farming villages and nodal sites, one in particular, were the meeting grounds wherein Cahokian society was born.

Hybridity

In diverse studies worldwide, analysts have grappled with how to understand the ways in which encounters between unlike peoples might engender dramatic social change. Historical anthropology and archaeology have most commonly looked to notions of "creolization" and "invented tradition" (Deagan 1996; Loren 2007; Silliman 2005). Most such studies have focused on colonial encounters or periods during which identities were radically reconfigured. However, such processes and encounters in the past were not limited to colonial periods, and the differences need not be on the geopolitical scale of many colonial encounters.

All encounters of any significant scale are complex negotiations that affect participants in some way (Lightfoot 1995; Lightfoot et al. 1998), and there is always some degree of difference that is subject to negotiation. Culture is always shifting and always in a state of becoming (Appadurai 1990; Bhabha 1990, 1994; Giddens 1984; Sztompka 1991). In terms familiar to archaeologists, this is the equivalent of saying that culture is a process, not a thing (Binford 1962). So, everyone approaches every encounter culturally, and the meeting of individuals is a meeting of those cultures. What happens then? The process must necessarily involve hybridity, which is to say the state in which cultural materials and practices are overlaid, assembled, syncretized, mixed, and hybridized.

Hybridity is more than the sum of its parts. While concepts such as creolization and syncretism can describe the creation of something new, this "something" derives from a borrowing of existing parts and generally does not explain why such encounters result in innovation. For instance, archaeologists might speak of hybrid pottery, say, a Terminal Late Woodland cord-marked jar that was tempered with crushed mussel shell rather than with grit or grog (e.g., Vogel 1975). This would be a case of mixing, such as taking a Late Woodland pottery trait and adding to it a Mississippian shell-tempered vessel. The result is a hybrid—perhaps a creolization or syncretism—in the sense of a combination of traits not normally found in either Late Woodland or Mississippian vessels. The traits themselves remain discrete, and there is little novel beyond the unusual combination (Alt 2008, 2010).

By contrast, the focus in hybridity is on invention. That is, the ways in which potters engaged difference around them would have affected their sensibilities such that, rather than passively copying a style or a trait, they may have created an entirely new form of pottery (Deetz 1996; Ferguson 1992). Hybridity is, in effect, the creation of something that may not reference its origins in any obvious way and that therefore cannot be reconstituted into those original parts.

From the colonial cases, we know empirically that such contexts are ripe with possibility. Hybridity produces unintended results and generates innovation. As Bhabha notes, "It is in the emergence of the interstices—the overlap and displacement of domains of difference—that the intersubjective and collective experiences of nationness, community interest, or cultural value are negotiated. . . . Terms of cultural engagement, whether antagonistic or affiliative, are produced performatively. The representation of difference must not be hastily read as the reflection of pregiven ethnic or cultural traits set in the fixed tablet of tradition. The social articulation of difference . . . is a complex, on-going negotiation that seeks to authorize cultural hybridities that emerge in moments of historical transformation" (Bhabha 1994:2).

Moreover, hybridities in Bhabha's sense could be read to suggest more than people. He is writing broadly about the spatiality and materiality of meetings. These are multidimensional entanglements involving objects, architectures, materials, nonhuman phenomena, and bodies of all kinds. Complex arrays of such things amplify the hybridity process. The otherness of subjects and objects has affects and can invoke particular sensibilities and lead to alternative courses of action (sensu papers in Gregg and Seigworth 2010; Stewart 2007; Tarlow 2012). Thus, we might speak of encounters between individual human beings or between things and people or between spaces and people. Indeed, hybridity can be found in everyday contexts and in all forms and materialities of culture. Accordingly, we might rethink the dimensions in which cultures are made and remade in specific contexts.

Memory and Ritual

It might help to analytically separate hybridity into memory work or ritual practice, on the one hand, and the affordant, agentic, or "vibrant" qualities of things and substances, on the other (Bennett 2010; Knappett 2004; Meskell 2008; Mills and Walker, eds. 2008; Van Dyke and Alcock 2003). Regarding memory and ritual, what people do and how they do it are inextricably associated with and shaped by the historical experience of a landscape and the places, bodies, and portable objects within it (Appadurai 1986; Basso 1996; Meskell and Joyce 2003). Any place, body, or cultural object is part of a continually renegotiated field or landscape of social action that takes material form and occupies space. Such fields have thick histories, with meanings that derive from those histories, which is to say the "genealogies" of practices, "biographies" of portable things, *chaînes opératoires* of technologies, and "experiences" of particular places, monuments, and architecture generally (Alt 2010:123; Dobres 2000; Kopytoff 1986).

For example, cloth has been said to be virtually synonymous with cultural identities in certain cases (Weiner 1992). The identities are literally woven into the physical and social fabric, such that weaving and wearing cloth projects the identities in social fields (Adovasio et al. 2001; Minar 2001). Other daily practices also project or inscribe memories and identities (Dietler and Herbich 1998; Fisher and Loren 2003; Hendon 2010). This is particularly true of what and how people eat either in private or in public (Dietler and Hayden 2001). Thus, practices, identities, ideologies, and regional-political complexes were always being creolized, hybridized, and remade both in everyday contexts and in extraordinary performances via habitual (or "incorporated") and discursive (or "inscribed") practices (Connerton 1989; Loren 2001, 2003; Rowlands 1993).

Of course, while people remember their own experiences, they do so imperfectly with the aid of inscriptions, mnemonic devices, visual cues, and so forth. Thus, social memories are subject to ideological negotiations, alternative interpretations, political appropriations, and forgetting (Halbwachs 1992). Accordingly, archaeologists have reformulated understandings of the processes whereby people identified with places or were subjected to the demands of central administrators and economies. Rather than assume that traditions, identities, ideologies, or cultural practices continued unchanged for centuries once they appeared, we understand them to have been continually remade, reimagined, or recollected through various sorts of inscription or embodied practice (Joyce 2004; Kus 1983; Mills 2004; Pauketat 2000, 2001; Van Dyke and Alcock 2003). Indeed, the idea of "community" itself should be understood as a fluid field based on collective memory work (Joyce and Hendon 2000). Community may seem to be expressed in collective rituals because that is where communal memory work is ongoing.

This work is happening at memory-making sites that might also be called "thirdspaces" (Bhabha 1994). Thirdspaces are the variably scaled entanglements where differences engage or the locations from which new cultural forms emerge. In thirdspaces, cultural authority might be recognized, scrutinized, questioned, and altered. Sign, symbol, and significance might be disassociated and new meanings might be negotiated. Innovation happens here; in fact it is unavoidable (assimilation in the usual sense is impossible). All sides of the meeting in a thirdspace change. All sides emerge altered. To variable degrees, something novel must emerge, depending on the scale and location of the negotiations (Bhabha 1994).

Specific events, such as feasts, funerals, house-building ceremonies, or other dedicatory offerings, might be considered in such terms. Any collective, commemorative event is a particular kind of thirdspace. Of course, collective events are both integrative, at the community level, and power-laden moments of local and regional culture building (Turner 1974). People might exploit the ambiguities of such situations to achieve specific goals. These situations would include political rituals, conventions, parades, presidential inaugurations, and so forth (Kertzer 1988). In these settings, people would also be subjected to a wider field of nonhuman beings, things, and spaces, making periodic communal gatherings especially important moments of culture making and innovation.

Cultural anthropologists have done a better job than archaeologists of studying the discrete ritual-performance thirdspaces at the scale of concern here (e.g., Firth 1983; Malinowski 1961; Mauss 1990; Turner 1974). It is in such contexts that identity, politics, and meaning are all at play (Kertzer 1988; Low 2000). In archaeology, the turn toward agency, practice, and performance in the 1990s led to notable studies that get at this same collective interplay, such as Rosemary Joyce's (2001) work on performing the body, Susan Kus and Victor Raharigaona's (2000) analysis of space and metaphor, Michael Dietler and Brian Hayden's (2001) studies of feasting, and Takeshi Inomata and Lawrence Coben's (2006) understanding of theatrical performance.

In the Southeast and Midwest, these included efforts to differentiate the ordinary from the eventful (Gilmore and O'Donaughue 2015). Of particular note have been studies examining the contexts and content of large-scale ritual feasts, on the one hand (Jackson and Scott 1995; Pauketat et al. 2002), and mound building, on the other (Knight 1989; Sherwood and Kidder 2011). In either case, researchers usually emphasize the integrative, communal aspects of both contexts rather than the creative, hybrid, history-making side of such moments (Kelly 2001; Spielmann 2002).

An exception has been the analysis of both feasting and mound construction at Cahokia. There, the great sub-Mound 51 feasting pit, dating early in the history of the complex, seems to show an interesting mix of ordinary and extraordinary or of sacred and secular materials, foods, and sumptuary items that Pauketat et al. (2002) suggested was foundational to the generation of Cahokia. Among the materials contained therein were bits of planed wood and great loads of burned thatch that they suggested were from the maintenance or ceremonial renewal of mound-top temples. The diverse mix of cultural dispositions brought to bear on such a renewal process might have had the unintended outcome of generating social hierarchy (Pauketat 2000). That is, while not explicit, there are inklings here of the potential dynamism of Cahokian ritual.

Affordance, Vibrancy, and Animism

Besides the memory work attendant to their specific spatial and material qualities, nonhuman beings, objects, places, and phenomena—or their substantial or elemental properties—have affordant, agentic, and vibrant qualities (Barad 2007; Bennett 2010; Hamilakis 2013; Ingold 2000; Knappett 2004; Knappett and Malafouris 2008; Mills and Walker 2008; Pauketat 2013b). Depending on context, they will affect other things, beings, and bodies around them. They will induce change.

It is not only nonhuman organisms that have some form of "agency" (Walker 2008); so do objects (Gell 1998; Gosden 2005). This may be realized owing to their affordant character—how their materiality impacts human movements—or it may be a result of their chemical and molecular properties or their experiential or sensorial affects (Barad 2007; Hamilakis 2013; Ingold 2000). Of particular importance for the present case is the link between such properties and the sensibilities of pre-Columbian Native Americans.

For many people around the world (especially in nonmodern contexts), the sensorial affects of things, other organisms, and places—what they are made from, how they move, and how they are spatially configured—engender animistic sensibilities (Bird-David 1999; Brown and Walker 2008; Sillar 2009). People relate to such nonhuman beings and objects by recognizing their affordant or agentic qualities as a kind of life force or spiritual energy. Among the descendants of Cahokia and their Mississippianized neighbors, there was an understanding that in some times and places, certain things might be "alive" or "animate," and that an invisible power was responsible for the enlivening or animation process (Bailey 1995; Dorsey 1894; Hallowell 1960).

One could imagine that there will be divergent effects attendant to contexts (thirdspaces) depending on the variably arrayed "encounters" with such nonhuman beings, places, and things. That is, the hybridity of the contexts in question will be contingent on more than people and their traditions, but also on the fields of nonhuman entities and their substantial or sensorial qualities. This is precisely what I will be arguing is the significance of key moments or events in the greater Cahokia region.

Producing Complexity

Combining the studies of material, memory, and ritual with those of newer approaches to animism and the affordant or agentic qualities of substances and things, we can understand Bhabha's notions of hybridity and third-space in a new light. Certainly, there is little reason to start with the proposition that complexity should emerge and emanate from single political centers, much less that Mississippian polities are adequately explained by invoking chiefdom models. Indeed, as we shall see in Chapter 2, there is every indication that Cahokia was never a unified, homogeneous community wherein ritual might have functioned to simply reaffirm identity or integrate an extant community.

This is not to say that there might not have been attempts to affirm or integrate community at local or regional scales. However, it is necessary to recognize that complexity, and specifically Cahokian complexity, was a concomitant of hybridity, by which I mean the particular biographies and affective or agentic qualities of things and the genealogies of people who created new cultural forms under novel situations of cultural contact. Across the regional landscape, both farmers and Cahokian ministers or administrators would have acted repeatedly to negotiate the fields of things, practices, spaces, and memories, effectively associating people, land, and cosmos with each other and, not incidentally, defining a new agricultural system linked to Cahokia. This was a continual process, as complexity was produced over and over again at a series of ritual sites and settlements throughout the region as people enacted or commemorated their identities daily, monthly, and annually. Let us see how.

2
Cahokia's Ritual-Residential Core

Cahokia was first described by Henry Brackenridge in 1811, but large-scale archaeological investigations of the place and its related settlements did not occur until Warren Moorehead's work in the 1920s (Milner 1998; Moorehead 2000; Young and Fowler 2000). Even larger-scale salvage projects began in the 1960s, beginning with Warren Wittry's excavations of Tracts 15A and 15B (Pauketat 1998a, 2013a). Other large-scale projects followed (Bareis and Porter 1984; Collins 1990; Holley, Parker, Watters, Harper, Skele, Ringberg, et al. 2001; Pauketat 1998a, 2013a). The FAI-270 highway mitigation work of the 1970s and early 1980s in particular resulted in the excavation and publication of large amounts of data pertaining to settlements outside Cahokia in the American Bottom floodplain (Bareis and Porter 1984).

These projects provided the basis for inferences of Cahokian social, demographic, and technological changes, beginning with the Terminal Late Woodland period (A.D. 900–1050) and lasting through the Mississippian period (A.D. 1050–1400). However, the ways in which Cahokia has been interpreted have varied widely over the last four decades. Beginning in the 1970s, analysts sought external stimuli rather than internal processes. The immigration of foreign Mississippians into the region and contact with nonlocal people were favorite explanations (Freimuth 1974; Hall 1991; Perino 1971; Porter 1969, 1974). Cahokia's Mississippian culture, it seemed, was too different from the preceding Late Woodland culture of the same region to have developed in situ. Perhaps, some thought, Mississippian culture was imposed fully formed from the outside (Perino

1971; Porter 1974). A modified version of this external scenario focused on trade from the outside. For instance, John Kelly (1991) thought that Cahokia sat along major transportation routes on a frontier border. To the north lay a fan-shaped area of interaction. Peter Peregrine (1992), Dena Dincauze and Robert Hasenstab (1989), and others saw that area as a periphery from which Cahokia might extract raw materials.

Subsequent research has failed to substantiate either the intrusion or trade scenarios (Emerson and Hughes 2000; Fortier and McElrath 2002; Pauketat and Emerson, eds. 1997). Moreover, by the 1980s, an in situ adaptationist paradigm had replaced both earlier trade and migration perspectives (Kelly 1980; Milner 1998). Around Cahokia, that paradigm found purchase in the large-scale FAI-270 archaeological mitigation project, which investigated small sites outside Cahokia (Bareis and Porter 1984). It seemed to the authors of that project's reports that elements of Mississippian lifeways had been in place before Cahokia's mid-eleventh-century transformation.

For many during the 1980s and 1990s, the notion of in situ evolutionary development went hand in hand with a simpler chiefdom model of Mississippian development (Mehrer 1995; Milner 1998; Muller 1997). If Cahokia had no outside influences or migrants that mattered, the reasoning went, then the most parsimonious explanation was a local-environmental one. Parsimony here correlates with low population levels and limited Cahokian power and influence. For example, the argument that earthen mound construction required relatively little labor, and hence only low-order sociopolitical organization, is commonplace (Milner 1998; Muller 1997). Consequently, both Milner (1998) and Muller (1997) have also argued that the creation of the Cahokian landscape need not be viewed as an accomplishment with wide-ranging historical impacts.

In contrast, Rinita Dalan, George Holley, and associates undertook a reexamination of the Cahokian landscape that began to call such interpretive minimalism into question (Dalan 1993; Holley et al. 1993). They considered the totality of landform reconstruction at Cahokia, from earth-moving projects involving the infilling of swales to the construction of mounds as more than mere piles of dirt (Dalan et al. 2003). They concluded that Cahokia was a series of complex engineering projects built during short-term events involving significant amounts of physical labor to achieve.

Their findings were consistent with Melvin Fowler's (1974, 1975, 1978) earlier sense of Cahokia as a complex, cosmopolitan community, a view that he held into the 1990s (Fowler 1997). For him, increased agricultural intensification and the concomitant population rise were the mechanisms behind the evolutionary trend to greater Cahokian complexity. He and others posited that the increased population and growing scarcity of resources required mechanisms of control, and he posited that Cahokia occupied the top of a four-tiered hierarchy of other mound centers and smaller habitation sites. He imagined Cahokia as the "first-line" community, with smaller centers as second- and third-line communities, and hamlets, villages, and farmsteads as fourth-line settlements.

Although Fowler never asserted that Cahokia was a state, other analysts did (Gibbon 1974). Patricia O'Brien (1989) even suggested that Cahokia was a "divine theocracy." In a similar vein, Alice Kehoe (1998, 2002, 2005) posited that Cahokia was the capital of a state with Mesoamerican relationships. As opposed to the minimalists and adaptationists, Fowler, O'Brien, and Kehoe were said to have "exaggerationalist" views (Milner 1998; Muller 1997).

As is often the case, neither side of any of the debates was entirely right or wrong. Indeed, by the late 1990s, interpretive focus had simply shifted away from the old intrusion, trade-based, adaptationist, and evolutionary scenarios and toward history, agency, power, and ideology. Thomas Emerson (1997a, 1997b) and Timothy Pauketat (1994, 1997) led this movement, while carrying over elements of earlier studies, and identified Cahokia's complexity in more historical terms, suggesting that (1) "community building" was participatory rather than compelled (Pauketat and Emerson 1999; Pauketat 2000), and (2) the Cahokia polity was as unintended as it was directed. In fact, Pauketat's (2001, 2003) "historical-processual" perspective is based on the principle that spaces and artifacts embody cultural processes and that culture is participatory.

Pauketat (2003) also emphasizes resettlement as one of the major historical processes implicated in polity building worldwide, and specifically in the American Bottom. However, unlike earlier-discussed migration scenarios, his version of migration does not cause the development of Mississippian lifeways or prompt evolutionary changes. Immigrants are instead considered a particular element in the greater process of Mississippianization. They contribute to, but do not cause, change (see also Cobb 2005). Ultimately, Emerson and Pauketat's agent-based, historical-processual perspectives provide a stark contrast with minimalist and adaptationist approaches to the question of Cahokia's complexity. They also provide a jumping-off point for my examination of both Cahokia and its rural upland farming outliers.

Table 2.1. Phase Dates, Names, and Affiliated Sites for the American Bottom Region

Period	Date A.D.	Phase	Chronological placement of sites mentioned in text
Mississippian			
	1275	Moorehead	Downtown Cahokia ICT-II Downtown Cahokia Tract 15A East St. Louis Emerald
	1200	Stirling	BBB Motor Downtown Cahokia ICT-II Downtown Cahokia Tract 15A East St. Louis Emerald Grossmann Knoebel Lohmann Mitchell Olszewski Range Sponemann
	1100	Lohmann	BBB Motor Downtown Cahokia ICT-II Downtown Cahokia Tract 15A East St. Louis Emerald Grossmann Hal Smith Halliday Knoebel Lohmann Mitchell Olszewski Pfeffer Range Sponemann
Big Bang---			
Terminal Late Woodland			
	1050	Edelhardt	BBB Motor Downtown Cahokia 15A Emerald Hal Smith Knoebel Range
	1000		

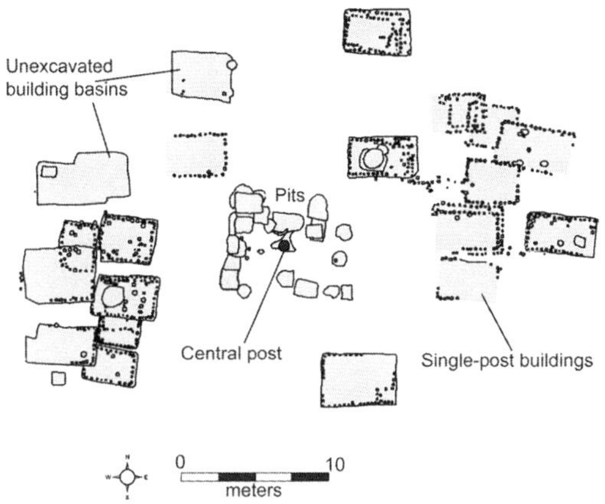

Figure 2.1. Terminal Late Woodland (Edelhardt phase) courtyard group, Tract 15B, Cahokia.

Cahokia

Between about A.D. 900 and 1050, Cahokia was far and away the largest village or contiguous series of agricultural villages and hamlets in the American Bottom (Table 2.1). There and across the region, farmers lived in small pole-and-thatch buildings arranged in groups of a few to a dozen around small open courtyards (Figure 2.1). Each household or courtyard group grew a suite of local starchy and oily seed crops, foraged for wild foods, and planted increasingly large fields of maize. By the end of that period, Cahokia had grown exceptionally large (Kelly 1990), with population estimates ranging to 2,000–3,000 (Figure 2.2). At those levels, Cahokia, even at this pre-Mississippian stage, was one of the largest human population concentrations north of Mesoamerica (Pauketat and Lopinot 1997).

During those early years, there was significant intercommunity and intracommunity diversity, judging from stone-tool and pottery assemblages. Indeed, the homogenization of that diversity is used as evidence to suggest political consolidation after the events that took place around A.D. 1050, also known as Cahokia's "Big Bang" (Emerson 1991; Pauketat 1994, 1997). Before that time, and based on excavated materials from the Merrell Tract, Tract 15B, and the East Palisade area, significant numbers of foreign-style Varney Red Filmed, Yankeetown, Dillinger, and Coles Creek pottery wares are known (Iseminger et al. 1990; Kelly 1980; Pauketat 2013a). The occurrence of nonlocal pottery has sometimes been taken as indicating an expansion of trade. Yet there is little to no evidence of material from the American Bottom found at sites where these styles origi-

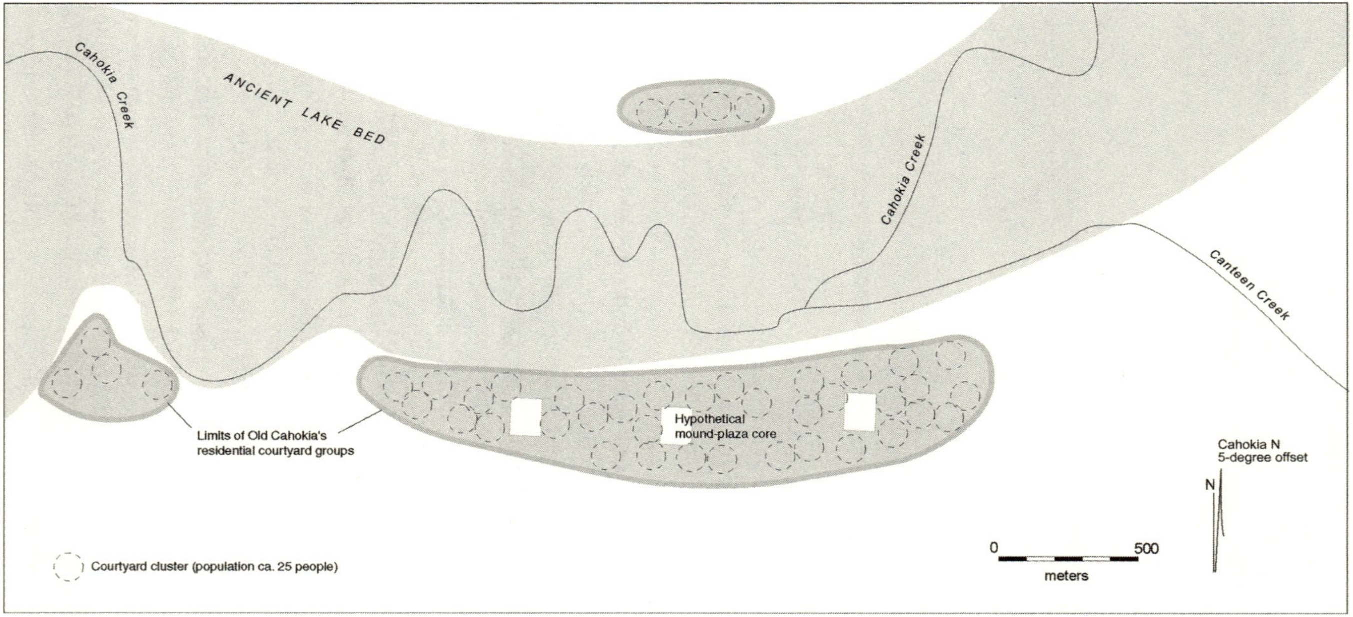

Figure 2.2. Schematic map of Cahokia, ca. A.D. 1000.

nate (Pauketat and Emerson 1997). For this reason, foreign wares are most likely indicative of distant peoples moving into the American Bottom region (Alt 2006b, 2008).

Whatever the causes, it is clear that after 1050 Cahokia was transformed into the largest pre-Columbian civic and ceremonial complex north of Mexico. By most estimates, at least 120 mounds were built within an area of 12 km^2 (Figure 2.3). A "high-density" residential zone covered an area of 1.8 km^2 within that (Dalan et al. 2003; Fowler 1997; Pauketat and Lopinot 1997). And within that, great earthen monuments take up considerable space. The large central pyramid, Monks Mound, has a base of 6 ha, which is comparable to or larger than the areas covered by the Pyramid of the Sun at Teotihuacan and the Pyramid of Khufu in Egypt (Figure 2.4). In addition, at 20-plus ha, the Grand Plaza fronting Monks Mound is large enough to contain most other Mississippian centers (Alt et al. 2010; Emerson 2002; Fowler 1997). These monuments dominate the central ceremonial precinct, sometimes called "downtown Cahokia," where the most and largest mound building, feasting, and mortuary events took place (e.g., Pauketat et al. 2002).

The cultural importance of this central ceremonial precinct is affirmed later in the history of the region, when, shortly after A.D. 1150, a large palisade wall was constructed around the principal pyramids and mounds of downtown Cahokia (Anderson 1977; Iseminger et al. 1990). The plaza was maintained until the end, although domiciles and other wall-trench structures encroached upon its once-open interior (Alt et al. 2010). But the atmosphere of the region had clearly changed, with the succeeding Moorehead phase (A.D. 1200–1300) frequently associated with the beginning of the end, if also a time that possibly witnessed some sort of revitalization (Baltus 2014). A possible biwalled palisade surrounded a portion of the East St. Louis precinct at the time, and a bastioned compound at Cahokia even guarded an L-shaped structure (Pauketat 2013a).

Cahokian Residential Areas

Up to and into this later Mississippian downturn, large areas of downtown Cahokia were intensively occupied residential zones or neighborhoods, as attested by excavations at Tract 15A, the Dunham Tract, and the Interpretive Center Tract II (Collins 1990; Holley 1989; Pauketat 1998a). Excavations at Tract 15A and Dunham (15A-DT) began in 1961 and were conducted by Warren Wittry, Robert Hall, and Charles Bareis in advance of a proposed highway interchange. The highway was ultimately moved, but the excavations resulted in an expanded understanding of the Cahokia site.

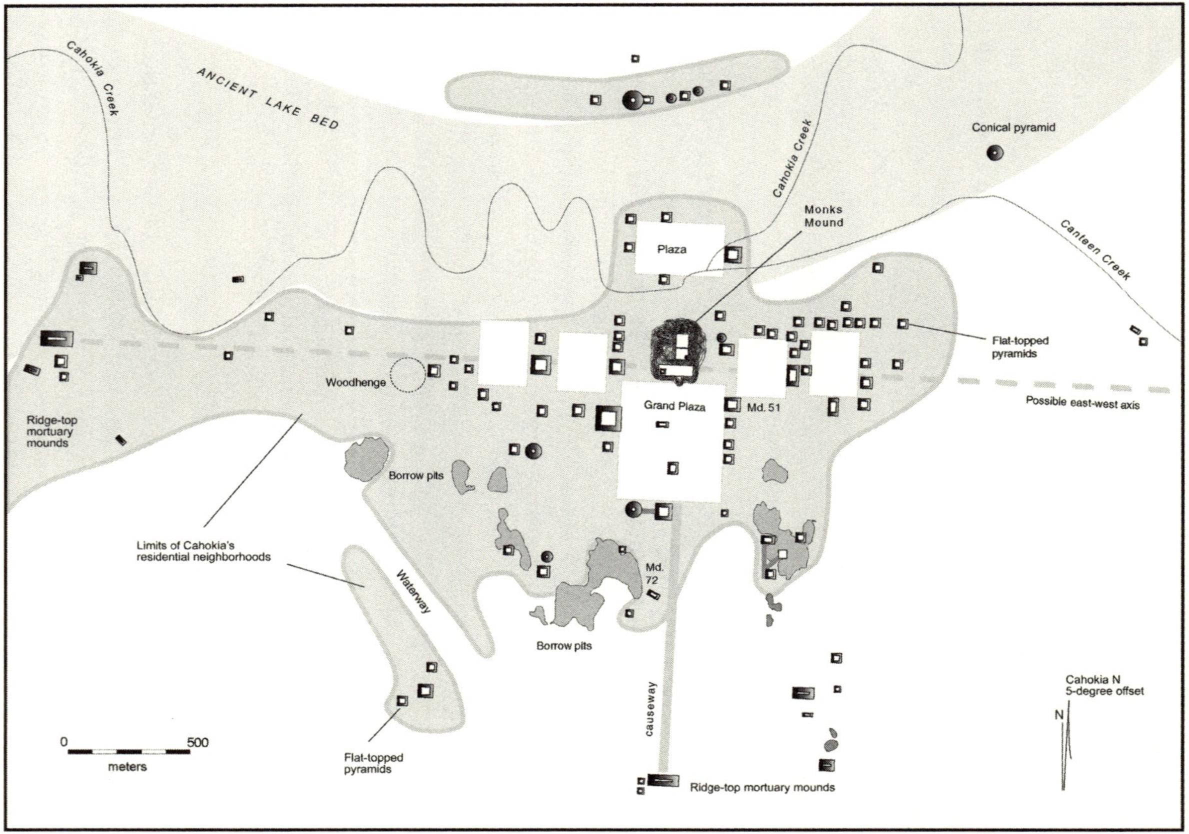

Figure 2.3. Schematic map of Cahokia, ca. A.D. 1100.

Figure 2.4. Aerial view of Monks Mound at the north end of the Grand Plaza.

Excavations of the Interpretive Center Tract II (ICT-II) were undertaken between 1984 and 1986 in advance of the construction of a new interpretive center at Cahokia under the direction of William Woods. Both excavations complement each other and provide baseline measures of human occupation of the innermost domestic areas of Cahokia.

At Tract 15A-DT, just west of Monks Mound, more than 800 features were excavated dating from the Terminal Late Woodland period, A.D. 900–1050, through the later Mississippian Moorehead phase, A.D. 1200–1300 (see Table 2.1). An abrupt transformation in spatial organization, architecture, and daily life is evident around A.D. 1050. The old courtyards were done away with, seemingly supplanted by a neighborhood plaza around which were small homes on one side, and slightly larger buildings paired with circular sweat lodges on the other (Figure 2.5). A few of the houses might have sheltered special artisans and quasi specialists who made celts (i.e., ungrooved axe heads) and projectile points or wove fabric. Such domestic zones contrast with the typical Lohmann or Stirling phase household, especially those in rural locations, which have been described as fairly homogeneous in terms of material culture, technologies, and architecture (Jackson and Hanenberger 1990).

Wherever they lived, however, people transitioned relatively rapidly after A.D. 1050 to building homes using wall trenches (Alt and Pauketat 2011). This is especially the case at Cahokia, where the transition was almost instantaneous in 1050, and less so as one moves away from the center,

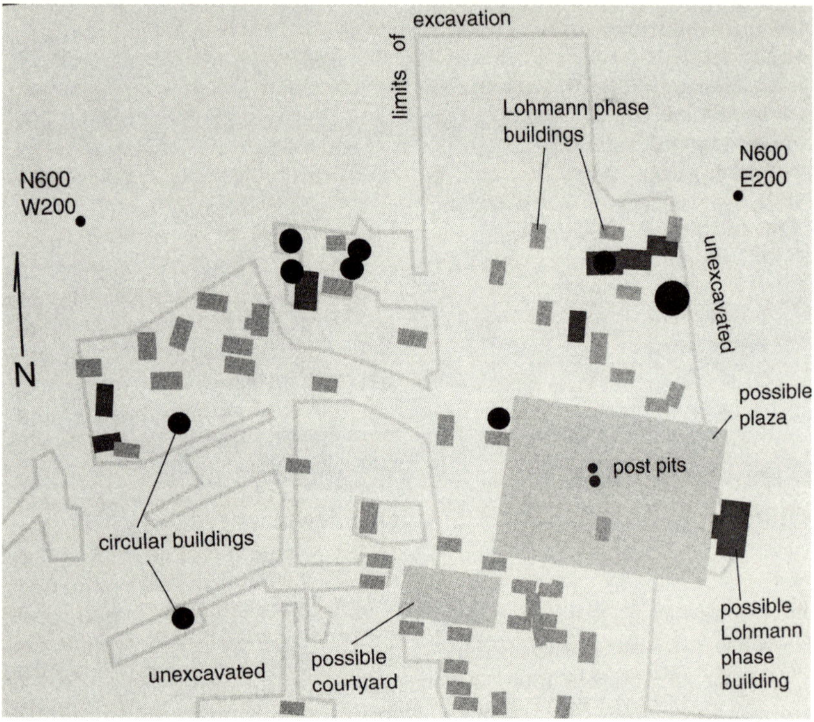

Figure 2.5. Lohmann phase subcommunity plaza, Tract 15A, Cahokia (from Pauketat 1998a; courtesy of the Illinois State Archaeological Survey, University of Illinois).

where single-post buildings remain common even into the early 1100s. Besides rectangular forms, wall-trench buildings after the mid-eleventh century included other novel constructions: circular sweat lodges and special T- and L-shaped buildings. These were often segregated from the ordinary rectangular forms. On Tract 15A, all the circular sweat lodges were clustered along the northern side of tract with the largest of the other structures. Later, oversized rectangular council houses or temples were built on the tract, as was a great post circle or "woodhenge" (Pauketat 1994, 1998a; Wittry 1964).

Cahokians in this and other portions of the central precinct most often used expedient chert-flake tools made from a variety of local cherts, if weighted toward a bluish-white Burlington chert, acquired in large chunks from the Crescent Quarries in the northern Missouri Ozarks, just 30 to 50 km to the southwest (Koldehoff 1987). The availability and use of Burlington chert surged after A.D. 1050 at the expense of other local cherts (usually available only in smaller nodular chunks), hinting at greater access or centralized redistribution of this everyday item. Mill Creek chert, which was imported as whole hoe, adze, and knife bifaces, also surged in availability after the mid-eleventh century (Pauketat 1994). With it seems to have come small amounts of other nonlocal southern Illinois cherts (e.g., Kaolin, Cobden, and Fort Payne varieties) used, in part, in the production of arrowheads.

With the chert, in turn, arrived minerals and crystals—hematite, galena, and quartz—and igneous rock. The rock appears to have been the detritus of celt production, with the raw material identified as basalt and diabase from the St. Francois Mountains of the Missouri Ozarks, just 50 to 100 km south of the Crescent Quarry area. This limited production of igneous-rock celts is clearly in evidence on Tract 15A-DT during the Lohmann phase, with hints that this production began a decade or two earlier (Pauketat 1994). In one instance, a single wall-trench building on the tract was found to contain two partially finished celt blanks made from the same igneous rock, a possible offering that, as we will see, seems to define what constitutes a Cahokian landscape.

Similar to the lithic tool remains, Cahokian ceramic assemblages were diverse and formalized, containing a number of specialized and utilitarian forms including cooking and storage jars, mixing and serving bowls, bottles, seed jars, beakers, baking pans, and a funnel form (Holley 1989). The decorated ceramic vessels among these forms, particularly some jars, bowls, and beakers, are thought to be related to ceremonial and religious activities, some more communal than others. For instance, Ramey Incised jars are considered a particularly Cahokian ceramic form, manufactured at Cahokia or one of its precincts or "ritual-residential" outliers. These embodied sacred meanings to the makers and users of the pots, and they appear to have been transported from Cahokia to other settlements (Pauketat and Emerson 1991).

Many of the same patterns seem evident on Cahokia's ICT-II (Collins 1990, 1997). Here, about 0.5 km south of Monks Mound and just off the southeastern corner of the Grand Plaza, was another Cahokian neighborhood. Excavations documented 468 features, including 142 structures. Though lacking a Terminal Late Woodland component, this portion of Cahokia was occupied from the early Mississippian Lohmann phase through the Moorehead phase. Neighborhood organization appears similar to that at 15A-DT, with structures organized in linear clusters and set at orthogonal angles to each other. Here also was a T-shaped building, two L-shaped buildings, and a circular structure among the other Lohmann and Stirling phase houses and storage buildings. Both the T-shaped and the L-shaped buildings were located at the southwestern edge of a neighborhood plaza around which other buildings stood as well (Collins 1990:129).

Among the living debris was a considerable quantity of Burlington chert debitage (as high as 98 percent by weight) along with low densities of exotic chipped stone materials. Concentrations of Burlington-chert microdrills are thought to be evidence of craft production, some of which might have taken place during ceremonial events (DeMott et al. 1993). The ceramic assemblage included a higher-than-normal frequency of noncooking vessels, particularly fineware bowls and beakers, compared to other American Bottom assemblages (Holley 1989). Ramey Incised vessels were present, if less frequent than at 15A-DT.

Other Precincts and Adjacent Complexes

Cahokia's central precinct and residential areas were flanked by a series of lesser mound-and-plaza groups and domestic zones (Fowler 1997; Pauketat et al. 2015). For instance, less than 10 km southwest of the central Cahokian precinct are two more precincts, East St. Louis and St. Louis, either of which would be among North America's largest mound centers if considered separately. The St. Louis site is separated from East St. Louis by the Mississippi River, but the distance involved is only 2.5 km. East St. Louis, in turn, was contiguous with Cahokia, with intervening mounds and likely habitation areas stretching along a narrow strip of land along Cahokia Creek and "Indian Lake" (Figure 2.6). All, it appears, were occupied simultaneously during A.D. 1050–1350 (Emerson 2002).

East St. Louis possessed 45 mounds and St. Louis included 26 mounds. Like Cahokia, East St. Louis has also produced evidence of the radical mid-eleventh-century transformation of the location from villages to an integrated city complex. Recent excavations there have revealed classic Cahokian architecture, technology, and material culture indistinguishable from those known at Cahokia proper (Galloy and Kruchten 2007; Kruchten and Koldehoff 2008). No evidence of significant differences or persistent conflicts between the people living at the different centers is known, although portions of the East St. Louis site were probably incinerated in the late 1100s as part of a planned politico-religious event (Pauketat et al. 2013).

As with the innermost plaza and mound complex of the Cahokia precinct, much of the interior portion of East St. Louis was not an ordinary

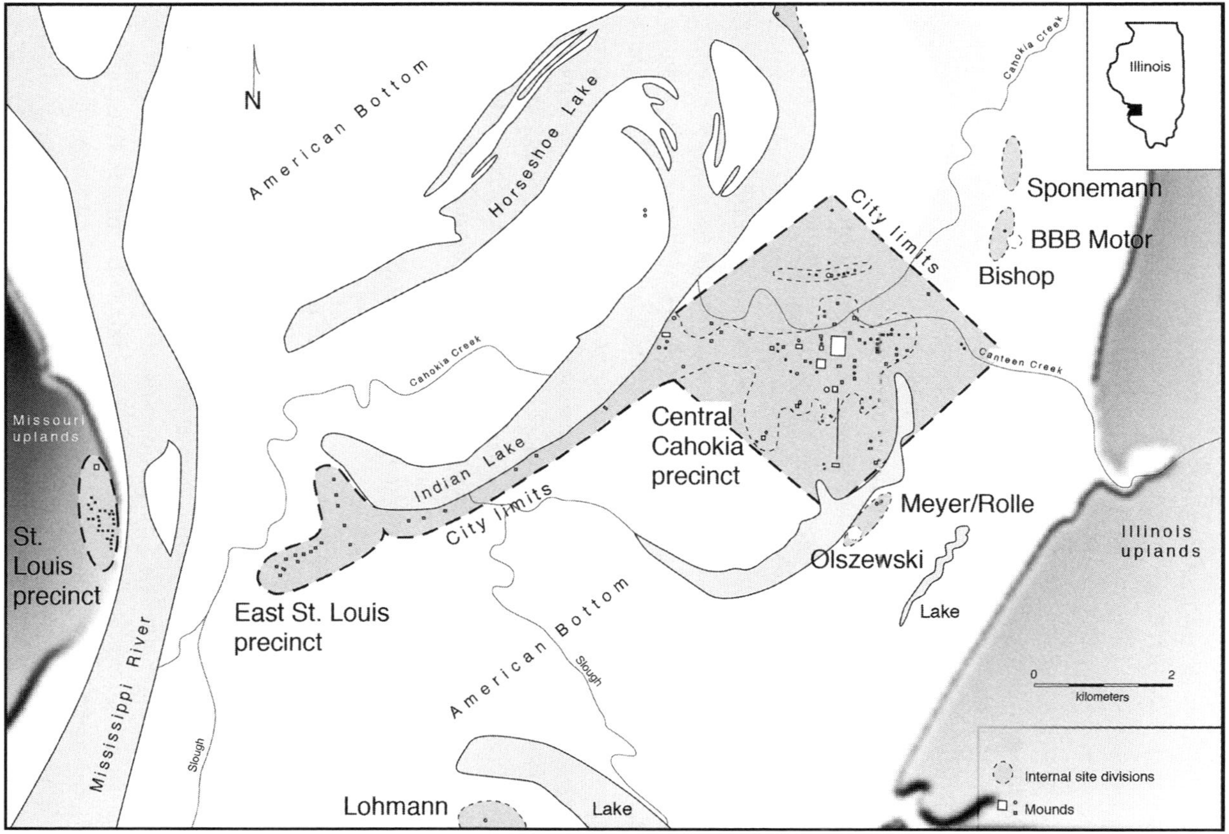

Figure 2.6. Cahokia's central precincts: Downtown Cahokia, East St. Louis, and St. Louis.

habitation zone, and we presume the same applies to St. Louis, now destroyed (Fortier 2007; Pauketat, ed. 2005). In the late 1990s and 2000s, a series of interstate highway–related excavations were undertaken at the site, the most recent resulting in the recovery of more than 1,400 pole-and-thatch architectural constructions: houses, council buildings, temples, T- and L-shaped lodges, and circular rotundas and sweat baths (Thomas Emerson, personal communication 2015). Two smaller excavations, on opposite sides of a highway corridor, are currently available for comparison, and these reveal what has been described as an elite or "ritual-residential" complex (Fortier 2007; Pauketat, ed. 2005). The low density of domestic debris; the mix of extraordinary qualities or kinds of other artifacts; and the extensive and dense sequence of wall-trench buildings, limited submound feasting remains, and other special buildings associated with two earthen platforms in one of these two areas—along with several scattered human interments of all ages and both sexes—led Pauketat to conclude that the "overbuilt and underused" area was home to a high-status family.

Beyond the Cahokian precincts is a series of lesser outliers, formerly thought to be "towns" or "secondary centers" within standard settlement models (Fowler 1978). These include several sites to the north, including Horseshoe Lake, Morrison, Mitchell, and possibly McDonough Lake and Grassy Lake. To the south of Cahokia proper, these include Lohmann, with the Pulcher and Washausen sites farther down the American Bottom often considered quasi-autonomous (depending on the time frame under examination). Of these, the Lohmann site is within a mere 4 km of East St. Louis and 6 km of Cahokia proper, and it bears similarities to the complex of Grossmann examined in upcoming chapters. This settlement of 11 ha contained but one platform mound, destroyed long ago during railroad construction.

The evidence from limited excavations suggests that the primary Mississippian occupation at the Lohmann site dates from about A.D. 1050 to the early 1100s (Esarey and Pauketat 1992). Excavations, limited to the southeastern edge of the site, exposed 14 structures. One of these was a rectangular wall-trench building interpreted to be a public structure because of its floor area of 44 m^2 and its unusual orientation. In addition, the building contained exotic materials and a portion of a human skull on its floor. Nearby was a second building containing celt-making tools, celt-making debitage, and a cache of four unfinished and oversized groundstone celts. Yet another very small structure, built with single-set post walls and with a floor area of just 3.1 m^2, contained an extended human inhu-

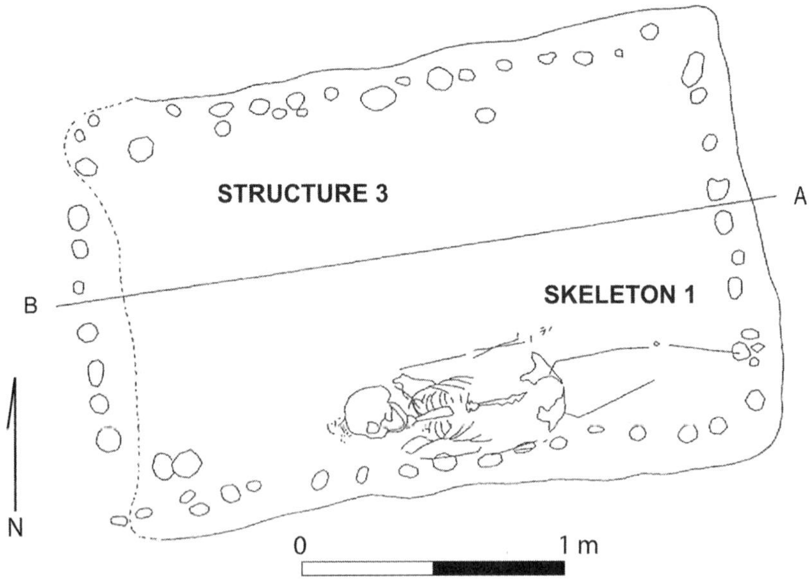

Figure 2.7. Plan view of mortuary building at the Lohmann site (11S49) (from Esarey and Pauketat 1992; courtesy of the Illinois State Archaeological Survey, University of Illinois).

mation on its floor (Figure 2.7). Its posts had been jammed into the ground to form walls, an unusual attribute possibly supporting the notion that it was specially built as a charnel house.

As is common in the region, ceramic and lithic artifacts betray a profile of seemingly mixed residential and ritual activity (Esarey and Pauketat 1992). Pottery jars—which are the most common type of cooking container known across the region—make up two-thirds of the broken Lohmann and Stirling phase vessels (65 and 61 percent, respectively). There were a number of vessels decorated with incised designs or effigy appendages, including Ramey Incised wares—special decorated jars presumed to constitute ceremonial wares made by a limited subset of the region's potters. Expedient flake tools and debitage made from Burlington chert, acquired from sources up to 50 km southwest of Cahokia, were common at 70 percent of the total chert artifact weight. Among the Burlington artifacts were 14 microdrills, 11 of these from a pit inside one of the houses. Other chert artifacts included broken pieces and resharpening flakes from Mill Creek–chert hoe and adze blades, imported to the region whole from far southern Illinois (Cobb 1989). These made up a quarter (26 percent) of the chipped-stone assemblage, with other exotic cherts from southern Illinois (Cobden and Dover) found in incidental amounts (less than 1 percent).

Most significantly, in 1943, an Aluminum Ore Company survey crew found a cache of about 50 unfinished celts at the Lohmann site. Reportedly, these celts had been placed in circular layers in a pit about 60 cm below the surface, 100 m or so away from the site's platform mound. Although the celts were divided among the survey crew and thus dispersed, one employee eventually donated 26 of them to the Illinois State Museum, and another gave 8 more to the Cahokia Mounds State Historic Site Interpretive Center. The celts in this cache, no more than blanks or preforms, were made from St. Francois Mountain basalt (Esarey and Pauketat 1992; Pauketat and Alt 2004).

Other Adjacent Ritual-Residential Complexes: Sponemann and BBB Motor

To the northeast of the Cahokia precinct are peripheral complexes or habitation areas that seem to be neither precincts nor simple villages or farmsteads. These include the Sponemann and BBB Motor sites, both of which have attributes virtually indistinguishable from those of Lohmann, East St. Louis, and central Cahokia (Emerson and Jackson 1984; Jackson et al. 1992). Excavations at both sites were conducted as part of the FAI-270 highway project and have been previously used to generalize about Cahokia's rural landscape. All were probably settlement units attached to or closely related to the downtown precinct. However, given the ambiguity surrounding the definition of Cahokia and its precincts and their relevance to the Grossmann site (Chapters 4–5), close attention to their features is in order.

The Sponemann site sits just 3 km north of downtown Cahokia. Its Stirling phase occupation comprised 12 structures divided into two distinct feature clusters (Jackson et al. 1992). One of the feature clusters is defined as residential, while the other is considered a "ceremonial complex" (see also Emerson 1997a). The four structures of the former were occupied at the same time as the eight buildings of the latter ceremonial node, which were arranged in a horseshoe shape. Features are interpreted to include a small rectangular temple, with single-set post wall construction, and a circular sweat lodge as well as typical rectangular wall-trench structures. Also included were six marker posts, a "world renewal" pit, and two related Green Corn pits (Fortier 1992). Material remains included extraordinary quantities of exotic cherts and "magico-ritual" items, a microdrill cache, and the remains of a ceramic vessel assemblage somewhat distinct from ordinary utilitarian pottery.

The chert and ceramic pattern parallels a Cahokian one, with exotics or extraordinary articles partially segregated from more typical domestic debris. For instance, common Burlington-chert flake tools and debitage accounted for most (81 percent) of all chert by weight in the Sponemann residential area; Mill Creek–chert resharpening flakes and hoe-blade fragments made up just 6 percent of the same assemblage. However, in the ceremonial area, Burlington chert accounted for less than half (47 percent) of all chert, while bits of Mill Creek–chert hoes and adze blades made up over a third (37 percent). Other exotic Kaolin, Dongola, and Cobden cherts in both areas were also known (ca. 2 percent) (Williams 1992).

Regarding the site's ceramics, it is noteworthy that the proportion of jars to other vessel forms is similar to if slightly greater than that at Cahokia's Tract 15A-DT or ICT-II (60 percent for Sponemann versus 55 percent for Cahokia). The residential node had a higher incidence of slipped vessels than the ceremonial node, and Ramey Incised vessels accounted for 20 percent of all Sponemann jars. There were at least five other nonutilitarian pots, including a white slipped miniature jar of the sort known from Cahokia's sub-Mound 51 feasting pit (Jackson et al. 1992).

There were also burned fragments of four carved, anthropomorphic flint-clay figurines from seven features in the ceremonial complex. Most figurine fragments were found in a burned temple and had been burned themselves. Of the group, at least two and possibly all four embody female characters (Jackson et al. 1992). One, shown with plant stalks growing out of her palms, is interpreted as the mythical corn mother. Another wears a skirt and is kneeling on a platform or basket with vines growing up around her; her position and the plates in her hands suggest an offering or supplication. A third figurine has a coiled rattlesnake crown on her head as well as snakes at her side. A fourth, highly fragmented figurine shows a carved basket thought by Fortier (1992) to depict a temple basket used to hold the bones of ancestors.

BBB Motor Site

The BBB Motor site is located just outside downtown Cahokia and across a low swale from the Bishop site, an unexcavated single-mound site possibly similar to the Lohmann complex (Emerson and Jackson 1984). The BBB Motor site as excavated consisted of two feature clusters. The southern cluster includes the remains of two pole-and-thatch buildings dated to the Lohmann phase, while the northern cluster of two additional structures dates to the Stirling phase (see Table 2.1). Both the southern and northern clusters are thought by Emerson (1997a) to be temple-mortuary ceremonial nodes. Their relationship to the Bishop site to the west is unclear.

In any case, BBB Motor's Lohmann phase component contained two buildings, marker posts, and eight burials. Material remains included exotic materials such as galena, quartz crystals, and hematite. The Stirling phase component comprised 64 features including a small rectangular temple, a sacred fire enclosure, a grave house (possibly similar to that at the Lohmann site), burials, screens, marker posts, and a "world renewal" pit. Burned mud dauber nests, likely indicative of the incineration of roof thatch, were found in association. Otherwise, Emerson thought many of the features were related to mortuary activities. As at Sponemann, the material remains around the temples and other buildings included exotic minerals and pigment stones: galena, quartz crystals, and hematite (Emerson 1997a).

As at Cahokia, Lohmann, and Sponemann, Burlington chert was common at the BBB Motor site, accounting for most (90 percent) of all chert artifacts by weight, much of it appearing to the analysts as high-quality material (Emerson and Jackson 1984). Unlike these other sites, the BBB Motor site had far less Mill Creek and Cobden chert debitage in the lithic assemblage (only 12 percent), with the usual incidental amounts of southern Illinois chert (Dongola) and trace amounts of local Ste. Genevieve and Fern Glen cherts. As at these other sites, pottery jars made up nearly three-quarters (72 percent) of all vessels, and Ramey Incised jars, in turn, made up nearly a fifth (18 percent) of that category. Other decorated containers were found amid the Stirling phase features (Emerson and Jackson 1984).

Also found amid the Stirling phase features were two red flint-clay figurines. One of these was found in a small isolated pit. Most of the other, in two pieces, was found inside a small temple. The first is a kneeling or squatting female figure shown tilling the back of a great serpent with a hoe. The serpent resembles a feline-headed monster, a motif widespread in the Southeast. Its body transforms into vines of bottle gourds after the goddess digs into it. The second figurine is also a kneeling female, possibly with deliberate cranial deformation. She has straight, long hair and, like the other, is wearing only a skirt. She is kneeling on what may be corn husks in front of an object that is now interpreted as a basket, likely containing the bones of ancestors. Both images are suspected to represent aspects of the underworld and fertility symbolism (Emerson 1997b).

Other Floodplain Nodes and Beyond

Given their special qualities, the architecture and flint-clay figurines among them, Emerson (1997a) describes both the BBB Motor and Sponemann sites as nodes of a Cahokia-centric network integrating the region's farming populace. He sees such rural nodal settlements as having been laterally linked to each other and serving various civic and ceremonial functions vis-à-vis Cahokia. The glue that held such a network together, he says, was religious ceremony (Emerson 1997b). Rejecting minimalist arguments that farmsteads were self-reliant and independent (Mehrer 1995), Emerson maintains that farmsteads were an official part of the Cahokian community, organized to a large extent from the top down and maintained through commoner compliance. The proof of such an organization would seem to lie among the remains of Cahokia's "architecture of power"—Cahokian sweat lodges, T-shaped buildings, and council houses—and the material symbols of Cahokian identity, if not authority, found at these sites, such as Ramey Incised pots, mineral crystals, and carved figurines (Emerson 1997a, 1997b). In a sense, Emerson sees the nodal and the non-nodal rural sites as constituents of a dispersed community pattern that integrated farmers with the centralized community of Cahokia.

In the floodplain itself, most nodal outliers are small, as in the example of the Mississippian occupation of the Range site. Located some 19 km south of downtown Cahokia, the Lohmann and Stirling phase components of the Range site include two earlier "civic-ceremonial" nodes and a subsequent "civic node." The Lohmann phase nodes contained a free-standing marker post, a large Green Corn pit, several sequential wall-trench and single-post buildings, and a large communal structure or "council house" covering nearly 60 m^2. The Stirling phase civic node comprised a series of sequential sweat lodges and storage or activity buildings, along with two residential structures and several marker posts (Emerson 1997a). Besides the usual scattered mix of domestic debris and exotica in proportions similar to those at Cahokia and the other residential-ritual complexes already reviewed, there were four ceremonially killed, or intentionally heat exploded, vessels and chunkey stones (objects associated with a game played in ritual contexts during the Mississippian period in the American Bottom) (Emerson 1997a; Hanenberger 2003).

Some have questioned whether such sites support Emerson's argument for a Cahokia-centric organization. Others have simply overlooked the implications of the nodal sites. If Emerson is correct, then we should also see similar sites wherever farming populations seem to have existed within a possible Cahokian orbit—minimally within a walk of a day or two from the central precincts of St. Louis, East St. Louis, and Cahokia. We might further presume that they should possess architecture, artifacts, and features similar to those at the Sponemann, Lohmann, BBB Motor, Range, East St. Louis, and Cahokia sites. This is in fact what we do see east of the Mississippi River floodplain in an upland area dubbed the "Richland Complex" (Alt 2001; Pauketat 1998b).

The Richland Complex is an apparent concentration of Cahokian farming settlements east of the floodplain that I have previously argued was populated to some significant extent by resettled or immigrant farmers over a few short years, perhaps a decade or two, around A.D. 1050 (Alt 2001, 2002a). I review this upland phenomenon in the next chapter in part to establish its character in contrast to the Cahokian precincts, outliers, and nodal sites just discussed. Then, I turn to delineate one more Cahokian nodal or ritual-residential complex in the midst of the upland farmers: Grossmann. As important as it is to establish the presence of Cahokians in farm country, the Grossmann site also leads me to entertain questions concerning the processes of hybridity with which I opened in Chapter 1. The meeting of Cahokians and non-Cahokian farmers at a series of sites east of Cahokia would have been akin to the kinds of cultural contacts better known from the historic era. Might these have been recursively related to the creation of Cahokian complexity?

3
Cahokia's Diverse Farmers

Between A.D. 900 and 1350 or so, across the wide expanse of Mississippi River floodplain north and south of Cahokia known as the American Bottom, were farmers. They hunted, fished, and gathered wild foods, of course, but their lives revolved around the fields in which they grew chenopods, amaranth, maygrass, sunflower, knotweed, cucurbits, and maize (Simon and Parker 2006). Maize was cultivated more intensively, if not introduced as a staple crop for the first time, at the beginning of this period, around the year 900. Throughout the so-called Terminal Late Woodland period, which ended about A.D. 1050, these farmers lived in scattered villages or hamlets, some dispersed from the main settlement in field houses or farmsteads. The largest such village area before 1050 had been Cahokia, as noted in Chapter 2, with its contiguous series of residential courtyard groups strung out along Cahokia Creek. Within it, there may have been a small, mounded core area or plaza similar to one known from the Horseshoe Lake peninsula a few kilometers to the west (Betzenhauser et al. 2016).

What generated the rapid changes of the mid-eleventh century? Importantly, and as far as can be deduced, none of the Terminal Late Woodland agricultural practices known from pre-Mississippian Cahokia or any other sites in the American Bottom changed markedly with the expansion of Cahokia into a great Mississippian complex in the mid-eleventh century (Fritz 1992). However, there were also many social changes in the rural countryside (Emerson 1997a, 1997b).

Besides the emplacement of nodal sites across the floodplain around

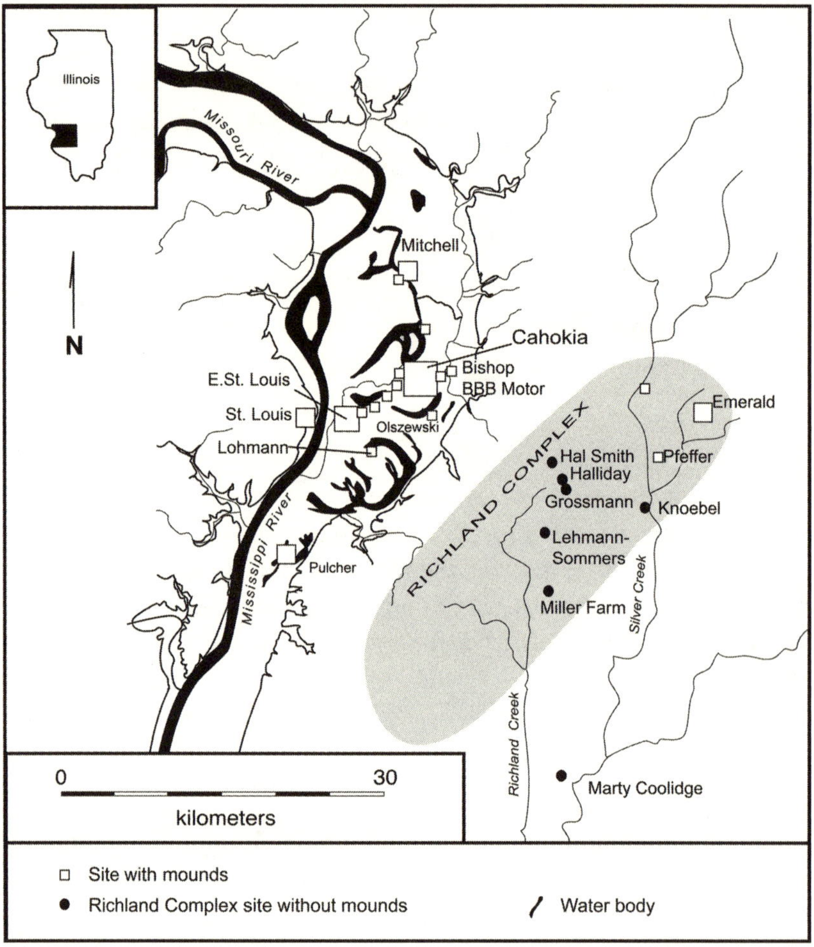

Figure 3.1. Plan map of Cahokia region, showing the Richland Complex and sites discussed in this volume.

A.D. 1050, as discussed in the preceding chapter, the most apparent social change in the American Bottom near Cahokia involved the replacement of multihouse hamlets and some villages outside Cahokia with single-family farmsteads. The pattern could not be any clearer than around Horseshoe Lake northwest of Cahokia, which has been surveyed nearly 100 percent for archaeological sites (Pauketat et al. 1998). From A.D. 1050 until A.D. 1300 or so, during the Lohmann, Stirling, and Moorehead phases, the typical Mississippian farmstead consisted of a cluster of storage pits, an outdoor activity area or two, and one or two wall-trench buildings.

One of the buildings might have been a living or summerhouse, while the other was a storage or winter home. Whatever they were, such farmsteads replaced the preceding village-style aggregations, tethered together into a vast Cahokian network via the civic and ceremonial nodes. Cahokians, it would seem, were ministering to or administering the farmers in the floodplain, who lived relatively peaceful, semiautonomous lives so long, one would presume, as they provided the appropriate amount of support to the Cahokians.

The pattern changes some as one travels downriver 30 or more kilometers, where the villages and hamlets seemingly remained on the landscape through the Terminal Late Woodland to Mississippian transition (Schroeder 2004). What about to the east? With the identification and excavation of similar early Mississippian sites in the uplands east of the American Bottom beginning in the late 1990s, the prospect was that the Cahokian phenomenon extended across that locality as well (Figure 3.1).

History of Upland Investigations

Mississippian sites were known to exist in the uplands as a result of pedestrian surveys conducted after the 1940s, but the characteristics of these places have only recently started to become clear. The most prominent of these was the Emerald site, with its 12 mounds, currently the subject of ongoing research (Alt 2016; Alt and Pauketat 2013; Pauketat et al. 2017). Secondarily, there was the Pfeffer site, with at least 10 mounds, a portion of which was excavated in 2000, 2007, and 2008 (Koldehoff et al. 1993; Kruchten 2000; Otten et al. 2007; Pauketat 2013b). Both sites were situated on prominent glacial ridges overlooking lower-lying outwash plains, and today both appear to have been "shrine complexes" (Alt and Pauketat 2017; Pauketat et al. 2017). Of these, Emerald seems to have witnessed intensive periodic ritual gatherings in which up to several hundred buildings were constructed for temporary use by visitors and pilgrims. Few permanent residents seem evident. Pfeffer, in contrast, may have had some permanent residents, though it too produced ample evidence of short-term housing (Pauketat 2013b). Analysis is ongoing.

In the vicinity of both is a series of other Lohmann and Stirling phase settlements without mounds. Some were identified during highway salvage work conducted by Charles Bareis in the late 1960s and early 1970s. Bareis excavated portions of the Knoebel village, as well as other sites (Alt 2002b; Bareis 1976). Additional excavations at the same sites found them to be at the center of an even more complicated landscape that included mortuary platforms atop adjacent ridges (Holley, Parker, Harper and Scott 2001; Holley, Parker, Scott, et al. 2001; Holley, Parker, Watters, Harper, Skele, Ringberg, et al. 2001). Multiple superimposed structures were found at all sites, especially Knoebel, indicating a permanent and enduring Cahokia-related occupation of the uplands.

Interestingly, despite the size of the Emerald and Pfeffer sites and the intriguing house cluster found by Bareis at Knoebel, archaeologists paid little attention to the uplands for decades. The consensus remained that the Mississippian occupation of concern when thinking about Cahokia was that of the American Bottom proper (Milner 1998). The presumption seems to have been that the uplands must have been sparsely populated. This presumption, one could argue, resulted from the biases introduced by the standard economic definitions of Mississippian culture used by archaeologists up through the 1990s. Mississippian culture was commonly seen as a floodplain "adaptation" (Smith 1978). For some, this meant that any nonfloodplain or upland sites, by definition, must be inconsequential. The Cahokia case instead demonstrates that a center may be defined, if not created, by its suburbs and hinterlands.

Most of the current data on upland Mississippian occupations derive from a series of excavations and surveys that began in the mid-1990s (Pauketat 1998b). Today, a series of villages, farmsteads, and special shrine-complex sites make up what is designated as the Richland Complex (Alt 2001, 2002a; Holley, Parker, Harper and Ringberg 2001; Holley, Parker, Harper and Scott 2001; Holley, Parker, Scott, et al. 2001; Holley, Parker, Watters, Harper, Skele and Ringberg 2001). Many dozens of additional settlements are known, some of which have seen excavations, and many hundreds more are likely if we extrapolate from the knowns, with an inferred human population of the Richland Complex that ranges from about 3,000 to 7,000 plus, not counting other upland areas in Illinois and Missouri (Pauketat 2003).

All such data indicate a densely occupied agricultural landscape during the century covered by the Lohmann and early Stirling phases (A.D. 1050–1150), with abandonment of farms and relocation of farmers thereafter. During their height, villages ranged in size from a dozen or so to 200 or more inhabitants (Pauketat 2003). Between them, as in the floodplain, appear to have been farmsteads, including a few with nodal architecture (Betzenhauser 2005; Holley and Koepke 2003; Pauketat et al. 2005; Pauketat et al. 2012). A general picture of who the residents were, and how they contrasted with floodplain farmers, can be created by looking at the lay-outs and materials of four extensively excavated Richland Complex villages—Halliday, Hal Smith, Pfeffer, and Knoebel.

Richland's People

Most of the sizable upland farming villages of the loosely defined Richland Complex were located on or near prairie or prairie-edge soils along Richland and Silver Creeks some 15 to 20 km southeast of downtown Cahokia. These are prime agricultural soils today, and they would have been equally as productive from the early 1000s into the 1100s (Benson et al. 2009). Notably, these villages were founded at the same time as the dissolution of large Terminal Late Woodland villages (in the floodplain and on the adjacent bluff crest) and the dramatic population increase at Cahokia proper (Emerson 1997a; Pauketat 2003). That historical synchronicity is all the more interesting when we consider food remains and the high densities of Mill Creek hoe-blade resharpening flakes: Richland's people were farmers, and some significant number of them likely overproduced to help supply Cahokia (Pauketat 1998b). Some of them were immigrants.

The Halliday Site

The case for immigrant farmers is made most clearly by a large three- or four-generation settlement that occupied the edge of the historically known Ridge Prairie at the headwaters of Richland Creek. Although at least a third of the site was destroyed or severely damaged by a modern housing development prior to 1995, the excavated portion of the Halliday site revealed the remains of more than 83 houses and 184 pits, arranged in seven courtyard clusters covering an area of 3 ha and dating from A.D. 1050 or just before to the early 1100s. A village cemetery was located immediately south of the settlement (Emerson et al. 2003).

The settlement's organization, comprising a series of adjacent courtyard groups, was similar to that of other Terminal Late Woodland villages in the region, especially Cahokia and Range (Kelly et al. 2007; Pauketat 1998a). Each courtyard consisted of an oval arrangement of houses centered on one or more central posts and ringed on the outside by activity areas and middens (Figure 3.2). Each courtyard group also possessed at least one small square hut, presumed to have served as a short-term storage facility for that particular courtyard kin group (Collins 1990). That each courtyard cluster was the living space and architectural constructions

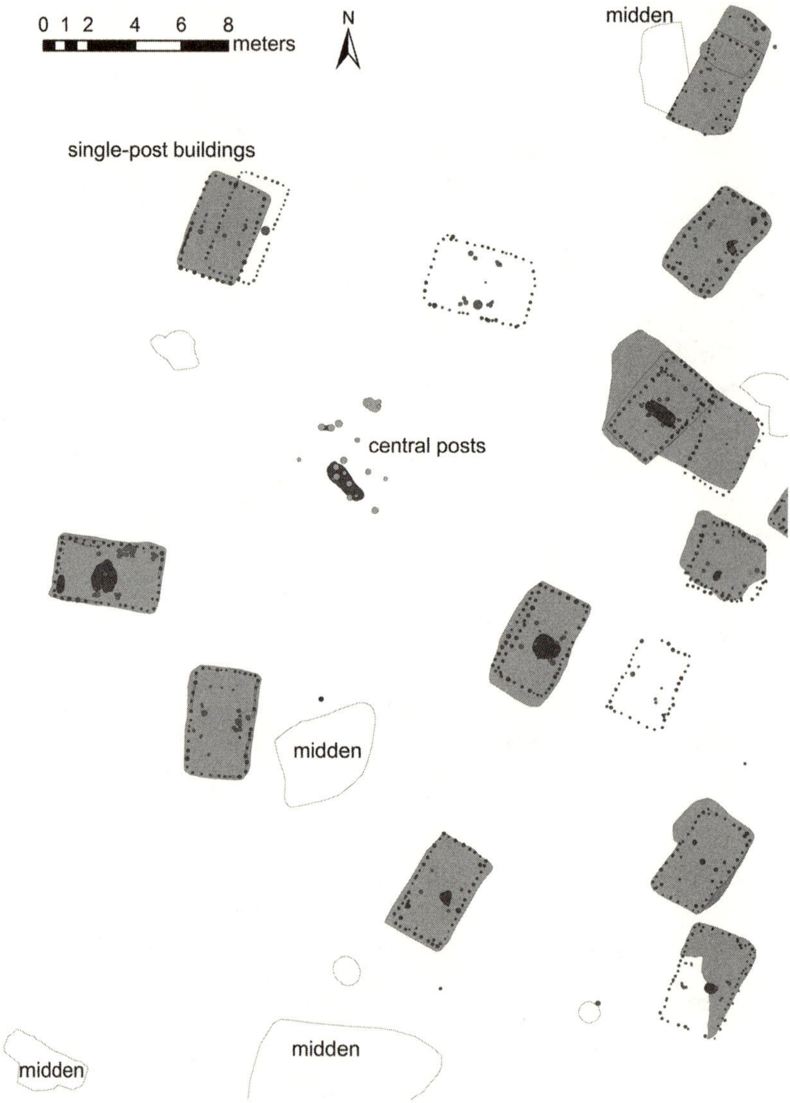

Figure 3.2. Plan view of a portion of the Halliday site (11S27), showing one courtyard group.

of a single corporate-kin group is supported by the pattern of house reconstruction. In every instance, the houses in any given courtyard cluster were built and rebuilt the same number of times.

In addition, most of Halliday's houses were constructed using the single-set post walls of the Terminal Late Woodland era rather than the wall-trench construction common to Cahokia after A.D. 1050. Even so, the average Halliday house was larger than the typical pre-1050 era pole-and-thatch home, falling instead into an early Mississippian mode. In addition, some were built in hybrid modes, using both single-set posts and wall trenches in combination, or single-set posts below faux wall trenches (Alt 2002a). Who exactly were these people and how did they fit into the larger regional picture?

Some insight into these questions can be gleaned from the site's developmental history. That is, the Halliday site was founded by a large contingent of people at once but was abandoned gradually on a courtyard-by-courtyard basis. The evidence for this conclusion derives from the inverse relationship between the number of times buildings were reconstructed and the density of domestic refuse in association, suggesting that while the Halliday site was probably founded at once, it was abandoned in a piecemeal fashion (Wesselmann 2000). Peripheral courtyards were abandoned first, with residents never having rebuilt their homes. Neighbors probably scavenged the old wooden poles for use as firewood. Certainly the remnant open house basins and pits they left behind became the dumping grounds for the remaining families' domestic refuse.

One courtyard near the center of the site had the least amount of refuse but the most frequently rebuilt structures. In that courtyard cluster, one building stands out. A rebuilt T-shaped structure, the largest at the site (7 × 3 m, not counting a 3 × 2.6 m alcove), occupied a central position (Figure 3.3). Within that courtyard, it was positioned near marker posts, storage huts, and deep storage pits. Just south of this structure was an unusually wide and deep pit filled with layers of burned material. A thick, greasy and ashy layer at the bottom of the pit contained a very high density of burned bones. The debris in the pit also included unusual pottery, as well as quantities of botanical material.

Preliminary analysis of the Halliday lithic tools and chert debitage has revealed two interesting contrasts with such material from people on the floodplain. First, Halliday refuse lacks exotic materials except for larger-than-normal amounts of Mill Creek chert (Pauketat 1998b). This chert arrived in the hands of Halliday people nearly exclusively in the form of hoe blades that were then frequently resharpened and, occasionally, broken

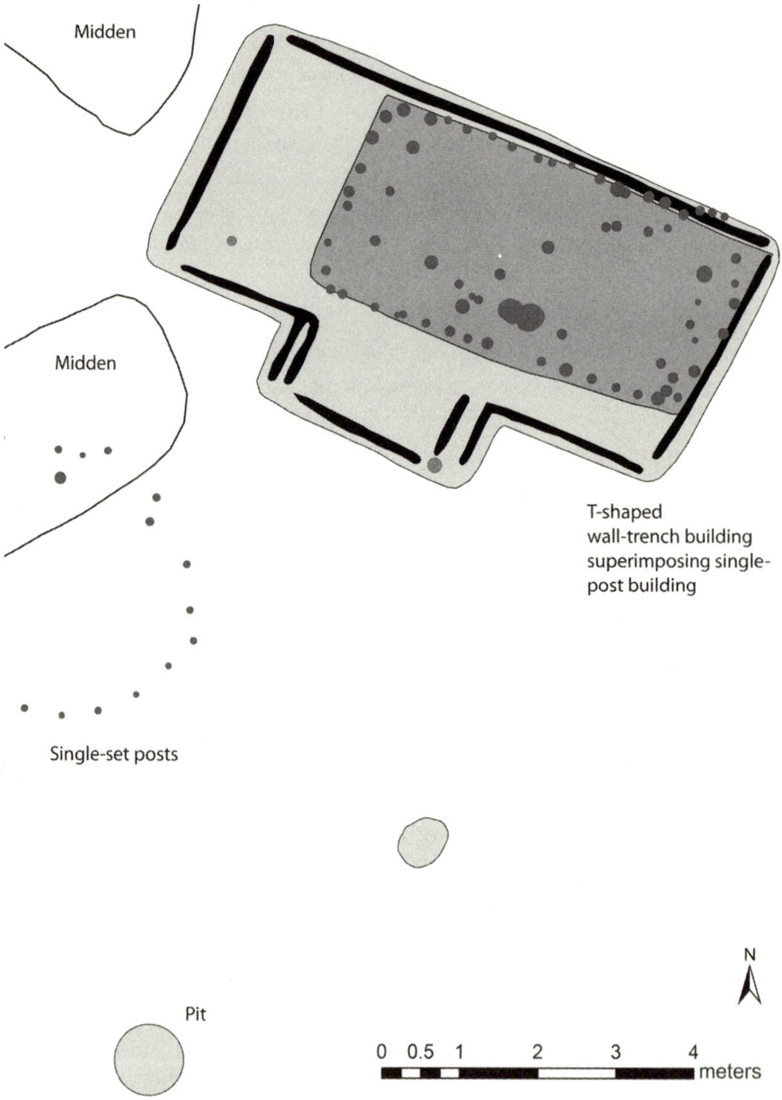

Figure 3.3. T-shaped building in the central courtyard of the Halliday site.

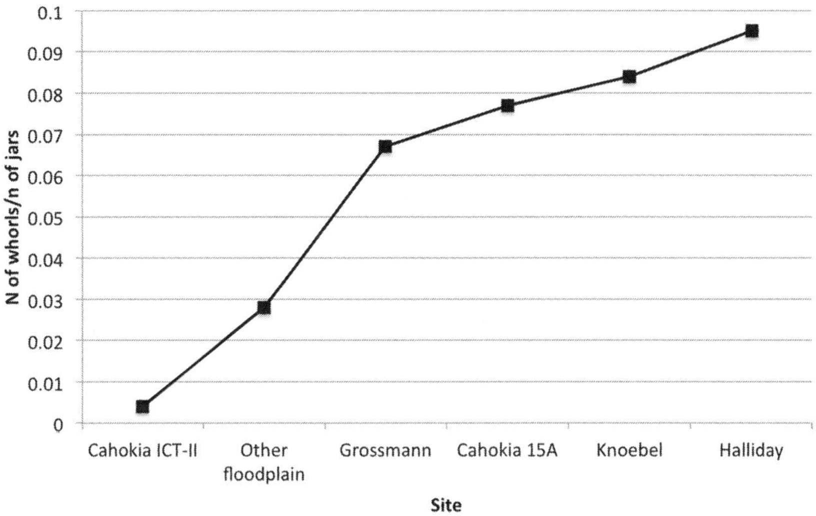

Figure 3.4. Density (number) of spindle whorls per jar from select sites (data from Alt 2002b; Emerson and Jackson 1984; Hanenberger 2003; Holley 1989; Jackson 2000; Jackson and Hanenberger 1990; Jackson et al. 1992; Pauketat 1998a).

and recycled. Second, both Mill Creek–chert hoe-blade pieces and the Burlington-chert flake tools appear to have been used to exhaustion, as if access was more limited than at floodplain sites (Koldehoff 1995).

The higher density of hoe-blade debitage at Halliday seems to be matched by concentrations of spindle whorls. These perforated disks, made from recycled pottery sherds, are found clustered in several features in quantities greater than any known in the greater Cahokia region (ca. one whorl for every broken cooking jar) (Alt 1999). The concentrations and high overall density suggest a village-level, if not also within-village, specialization in cordage/thread or even fabric production (Figure 3.4).

The diet of the Halliday residents was also unusual as compared to that of floodplain residents. On one hand, residue analysis on pottery sherds suggests a higher reliance on corn than has been identified at floodplain sites (Beehr and Ambrose 2007; Reber and Evershed 2006). On the other hand, more small animals, reptiles, and amphibians appear in the faunal assemblage than have been seen at any other American Bottom site (Kelly 2000). Possibly, these dietary differences indicate a population ethnically distinct from that of the American Bottom region.

Such an inference is bolstered by the pottery remains. Although the clays used to make most of the pots appear to have been mined from locally available silty loess and till, there are noticeable differences in ce-

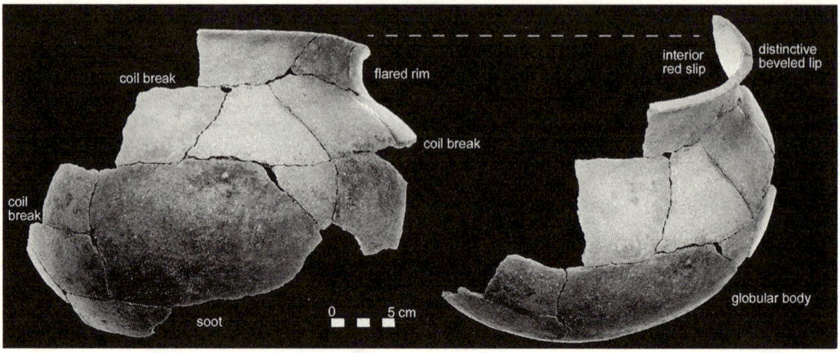

Figure 3.5. Views of a Varney Red Filmed jar from the Halliday site.

ramic styles and technologies as compared to contemporary settlements in the floodplain, differences that I have argued elsewhere were based on the nonlocal origins of many residents (Alt 2006a, 2008). For one thing, the Halliday potters relied on crushed mussel shell as a tempering agent more frequently than did Cahokians, whose pottery-making tradition was based on the use of grog, and later, shell. A total of 87 percent of all Halliday vessels were shell tempered, while the number was lower at Cahokia. The early Lohmann phase Tract 15A-DT assemblage consisted of 58 percent shell-tempered vessels, and at ICT-II, 73 percent of vessels were shell tempered (Pauketat 1998b; Holley 1989).

Just as significant is that pottery styles at the Halliday site included greater than expected quantities of nonlocal types. Primarily, these included local variants of Varney Red Filmed pottery, usually found only in southeastern Missouri and northeastern Arkansas (Morse and Morse 1983; Williams 1954). Such pottery was evident at Cahokia in minor quantities, usually less than 3 percent, but more than 30 percent of the Halliday jars alone can be classified as Varney (Howe 2000) (Figure 3.5). Minor amounts of Yankeetown and French Fork Incised ceramics, from southwestern Indiana and western Mississippi or Arkansas, respectively, were also found in Halliday village middens. Similarly, minor amounts of a locally distinctive type of Terminal Late Woodland "Bluff" pottery were also found (notes on file, University of Illinois). These were made with "Madison County Shale" clays originating 20 to 50 km north of Halliday (Porter 1984).

The Hal Smith Site

The Hal Smith site, located only 2 km north of the contemporary Halliday settlement, covers an area of about 2 ha. Within one 1,261 m^2 exca-

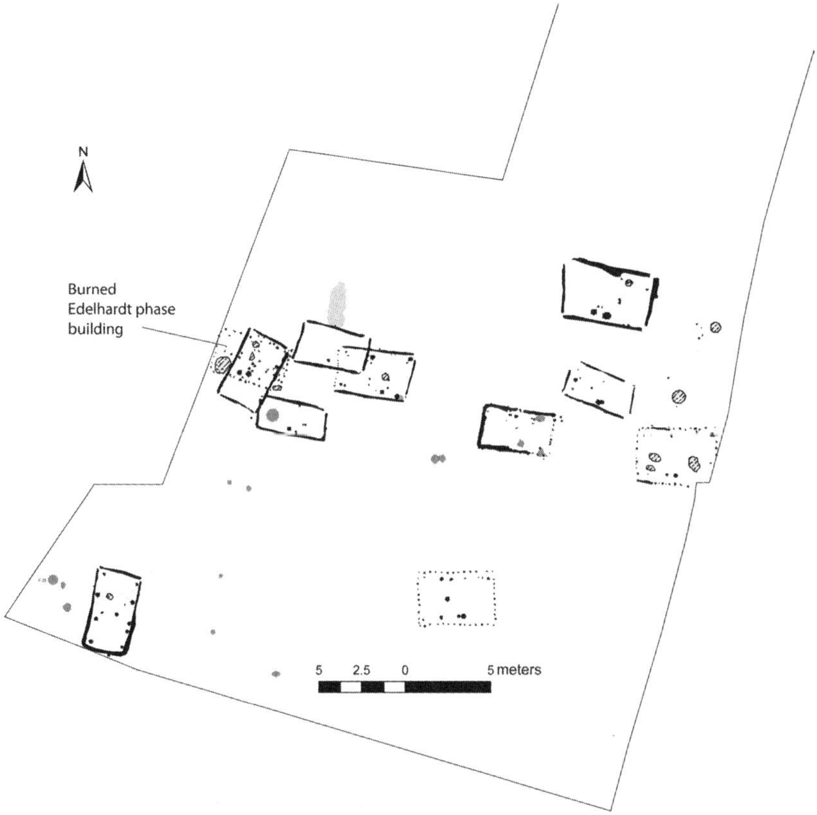

Figure 3.6. Plan view of a portion of the Hal Smith site (11S825).

vation block, 11 structures and 17 pits were documented (Figure 3.6). Of the buildings, one dates to the Edelhardt phase, and the rest were built during the Lohmann through early Stirling phases. Of the 16 Mississippian buildings, one was constructed using single-set posts, and two were built using both pre-Mississippian single-post and Mississippian wall-trench construction. The rest were wall-trench buildings.

Unlike the organically rich fills at the Halliday site, feature fills in the excavated features at Hal Smith were fairly sterile, with comparatively little ceramic and lithic material present. The fragments of the 26 recovered ceramic vessels compare well stylistically with Cahokian vessels, with some attribute exceptions, but not with the Halliday pots. For example, as at the other upland sites, Hal Smith vessels had less rim modification, as indicated by a high "lip-protrusion" index (Howe 2000). Hal

Smith pots were tempered with shell 74 percent of the time, comparing well with Cahokia's ICT-II figure of 73 percent. But there were no Varney Red Filmed, Yankeetown, or Coles Creek vessels similar to those at the Halliday site. In short, the high incidence of wall-trench buildings and Cahokia-style pottery makes Hal Smith look much more similar to Cahokia than to Halliday. The low density of refuse, again compared to Halliday, suggests either ethnic differences surrounding garbage disposal or an intermittent use of the Hal Smith site by people not related to those just an hour's walk to the south.

The Pfeffer Site

All things being equal, one might expect intermittently occupied sites in the same vicinity to look similar. However, the Pfeffer site puts the lie to that assumption. Pfeffer was a large settlement centered on 10 modest-sized earthen mounds located 9 km east of both Halliday and Hal Smith. As at Halliday and Hal Smith, the Mississippian occupation of Pfeffer dates from the Lohmann through the early Stirling phase. Originally covering an estimated 5 ha, the site has been heavily impacted by modern housing developments, a golf course, and a road that now bisects the site. A central platform mound and isolated portions of habitation areas remain intact outside the 2,000 m^2 area excavated in 2000, 2007, and 2008 (Figure 3.7). In that area are 39 early Mississippian houses, built in both single-post and wall-trench modes, and about 20 coeval pits (notes on file, University of Illinois).

The remains of four exceptional single-post structures sit south of the site's main mound and presumed plaza. Two of these buildings are characteristic of Cahokia's nodal "architecture of power" (Emerson 1997a). One is a T-shaped structure surrounded by six yellow-plastered pits. A second, a few meters away, is a circular sweat lodge. In a pit in between these structures was an apparent offering of an unfinished celt similar to those known from the Cahokia and Lohmann sites.

The other two exceptional buildings were of a type unknown at Halliday and Hal Smith or, for that matter, at Cahokia and other floodplain sites. These two large single-post structures had deep basins and unusual yellow-and-black-plastered floors. The material deposited in them, and the manner of that deposition, suggest that these buildings were sites of ritual activity even after being decommissioned and infilled. The smaller building measured 3 × 6 m and had two stacked yellow-and-black-plastered floors and formal hearths. Its fill was rich with artifacts interspersed between

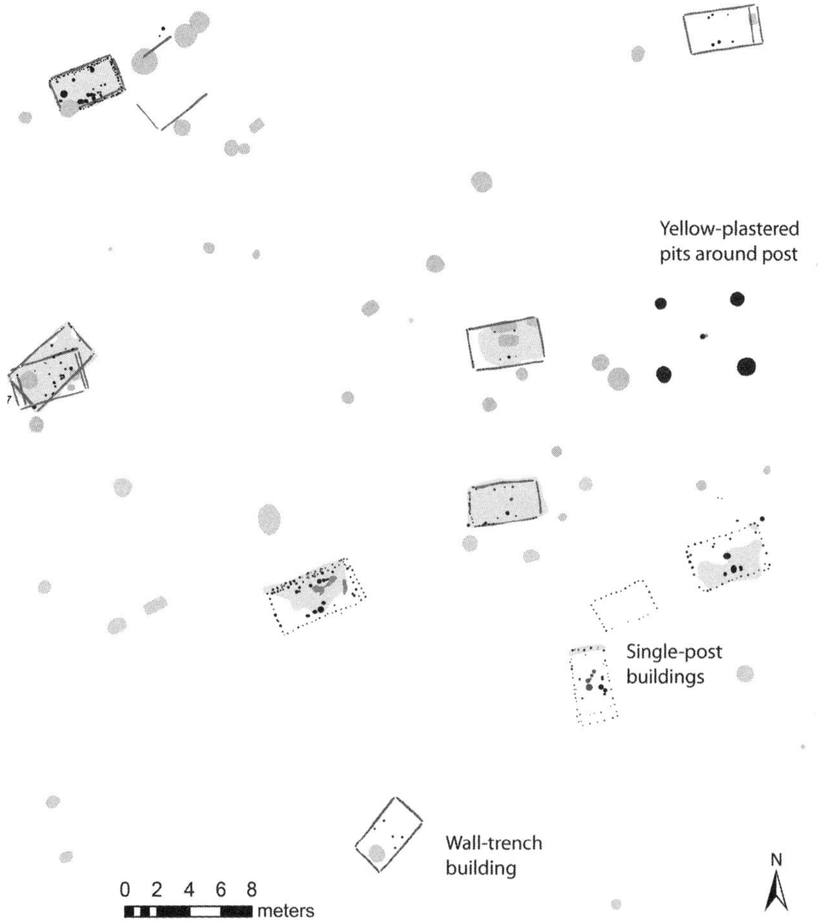

Figure 3.7. Plan view of a portion of the Pfeffer site (11S204).

sterile water-laid zones (Pauketat 2013b). The larger building measured 8 × 4 m and, subsequent to its decommissioning, was filled with burned and water-laid sediments in turn embedded with burned corn, red cedar wood, tobacco, hematite, quartz crystals, and two broken chunkey stones. At some point, Lohmann phase people had reexcavated the basin prior to refilling it with more special refuse. Five yellow-and-black-lined pits surrounded this building, the contents of which have yet to be analyzed.

Although the analysis of the ceramic and lithic artifacts associated with these buildings is, as of this writing, unfinished, Cahokian styles of Lohmann and early Stirling phase wares predominated in the assemblage, which lacked the Varney Red Filmed vessels so common at Halliday. Also unlike the case at Halliday, a large concentration of microliths made from Burlington chert was recovered from a wall-trench building at the site excavated in the 1980s (Koldehoff et al. 1993). Microdrills and microlithic cores are associated with shell-bead production at Cahokia (Holley 1995; Pauketat 1993; Yerkes 1983). In the uplands, few locations produced microdrills, although one such place was the Lehman-Somers site, a yet-to-be-reported upland village excavation 4 km southwest of Halliday where approximately 30 Lohmann and early Stirling phase houses were uncovered (Kinsella 2002). More than 800 microlithic tools and pieces of debitage were recovered in concentrations associated with one or more of those buildings.

The Knoebel Site

No microliths were found at the Knoebel site, located along the banks of Silver Creek 4 km south of Pfeffer and 7 to 9 km east-southeast of Halliday and Hal Smith, respectively (see Figure 3.1). This site, which covers about 1 ha, witnessed large-scale investigations in 1967–1969 in advance of highway construction, with additional excavations in both 1993 and 2004–2005. In total, more than 16,000 m^2 were exposed, within which were 33 structures and 68 pits (Figures 3.8 and 3.9). My reanalysis of Bareis's excavations identified a continuous late Edelhardt through early Stirling phase occupation, comparable to that at Hal Smith (Alt 2002b).

Like the pottery at Hal Smith, Knoebel's pottery was more comparable to that made in the American Bottom than to that at Halliday or Pfeffer, which seems to correlate with Knoebel's rapid transition from post-wall to wall-trench buildings in the mid-eleventh century. Its expedient chert tools and debitage were unremarkable. As at Halliday, however, the settlement's courtyard organization seems to have been unaffected by that Cahokia-inspired change. A post marked the center of opposing buildings both before and after A.D. 1050, just as it had for Terminal Late Woodland people living in the floodplain.

Yet the Knoebel site is singular with respect to its architectural remains. Beginning with the Lohmann phase, when numbers of buildings surged at the site, a series of constructions assumed an L-shaped plan. A total of 9 of the 33 buildings—including the central buildings of the hamlet—took the L shape, created when an additional room was added to the otherwise rectangular building. While room extensions were known at other Lohmann and Stirling phase sites, the Knoebel room extensions were more nu-

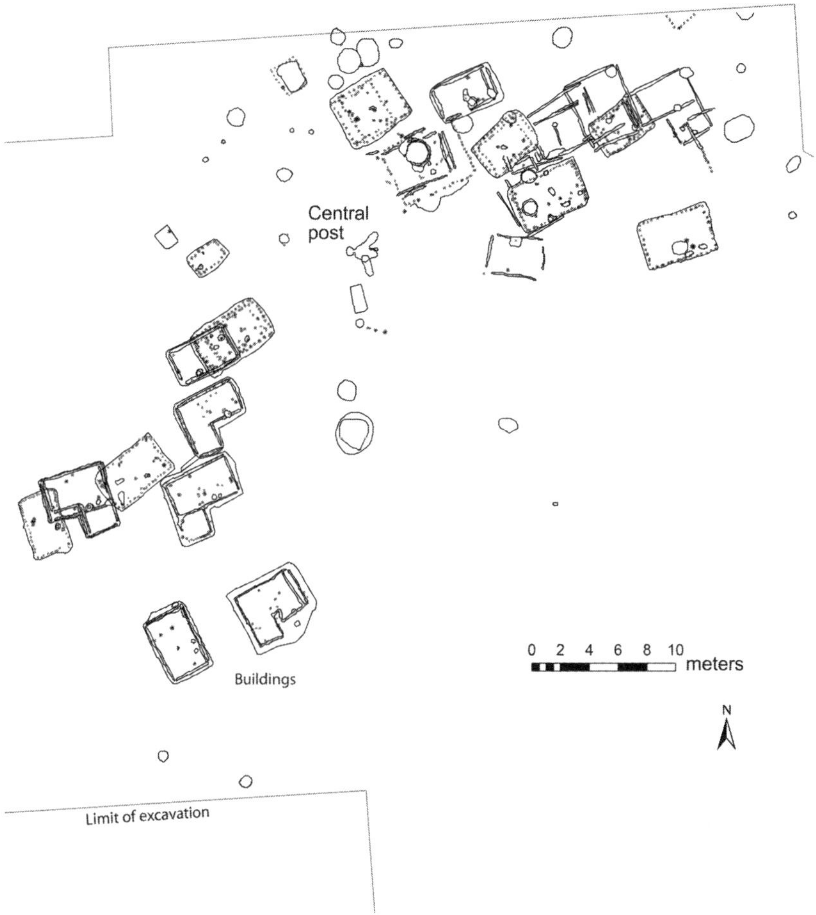

Figure 3.8. Plan view of northern portion of the Knoebel site (11S71) (adapted from Bareis 1976 and Holley, Parker, Watters, Harper, Skele, Ringberg, Brown, and Booth 2001; courtesy of the Illinois State Archaeological Survey, University of Illinois).

merous and larger than any identified elsewhere (see Collins 1990; Pauketat 1998b). For example, only 2 percent of Lohmann phase structures at Cahokia's ICT-II or 15A-DT were L-shaped, and one of the former had a larger room similar to that at Knoebel (Collins 1990; Pauketat 1998b).

The purposes of Knoebel's L-shaped room extensions are unclear, though they could have been used for general storage, not unlike the square huts at Halliday. As it turns out, the floor areas enclosed by the L additions at Knoebel compare favorably with the floor areas of the Halliday storage

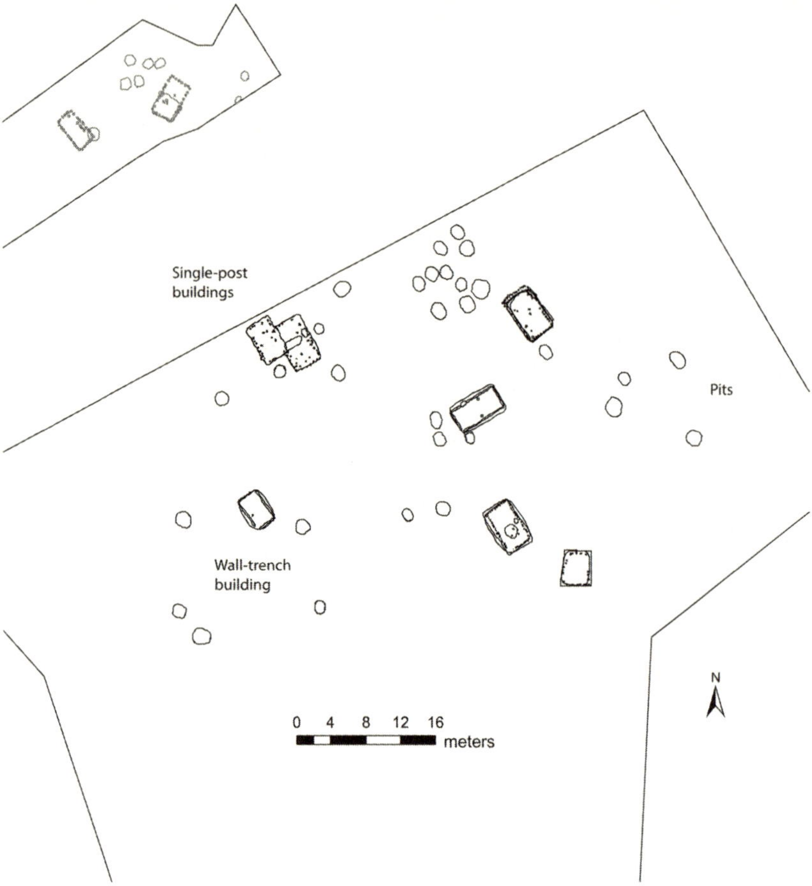

Figure 3.9. Plan view of southern portion of the Knoebel site (adapted from Bareis 1976 and Holley, Parker, Watters, Harper, Skele, Ringberg, Brown, and Booth 2001; courtesy of the Illinois State Archaeological Survey, University of Illinois).

structures. Moreover, Knoebel's L additions might constitute the numerical equivalent of one storage structure for every seven buildings, a ratio comparable to that found at Halliday (Alt 2002a).

Knoebel's hybrid mix of Cahokian and non-Cahokian qualities carries over into its other material assemblages. For instance, though lacking a microlithic assemblage, one building basin did contain percussion flakes associated with the manufacture of at least one celt (Kruchten 2012). In addition, one unfinished celt was left behind in a pit (Alt 2002b). Jar rim shapes, temper use, and vessel sizes at Knoebel follow Cahokian trends, but, as at Halliday, ceramic spindle whorls were found in significant quantities (Alt 2002b). Overall, Knoebel's pottery, lithics, and architecture—minus the L-shaped room extensions—more closely resemble those of floodplain sites than those at other Richland Complex settlements. Possibly, this is because of its deeper, Edelhardt phase ties to the people there, as at Hal Smith.

Complicating the question of their identity, 5 percent of the ceramics at Knoebel were Yankeetown decorated wares, a style originating in the Wabash valley of southwestern Indiana (Alt 2002b). No other site in the region, including Cahokia, had more than 1 percent Yankeetown decorated wares (some Yankeetown sites in Indiana had only 20 percent decorated wares) (Blasingham 1965). It is possible that Knoebel, like Halliday, was home to nonlocal people.

Discussion

As can be seen from the selected site summaries, settlements in the uplands differed in notable ways both from those in the floodplain around Cahokia and from each other. This difference could easily be read as cultural diversity, a possibility made likely by the fact that Hal Smith and Knoebel were founded during the late Edelhardt phase, after A.D. 1000, and the Halliday and Pfeffer residents appeared nearer 1050. Presumably, each village population came from a different location or a different time, accentuating a founder effect. Precisely where they originated remains uncertain, although the particular mix of characteristics exhibited by each argues for a highly variable upland cultural landscape (Table 3.1).

Certainly, people had been on the move in the years leading up to, and presumably during, this period. Emerson (1997a, 1997b) has made the argument that farm families were relocated from villages to farmsteads at the beginning of the Lohmann phase, presumably to support the larger project that was Cahokia. In the uplands, the variable organizational, architectural, and technological practices in evidence, even considering the data in qualitative terms only, would suggest less overarching control by Cahokians or, perhaps, a different order of administration. Perhaps the hints of intermittent occupations at Pfeffer and Hal Smith are related to alternative forms of management (or lack thereof).

Regardless, after their arrival, most Richland Complex settlers farmed, as indicated by relatively dense deposits of Mill Creek–chert hoe-blade maintenance debitage at the permanent settlements of Halliday and Knoebel. A few people at each settlement were probably responsible for craft

Table 3.1. Architectural and Material Attributes of Select Sites

	Cahokian buildings			Terminal Late Woodland features		Foreign pottery		Specialized productions			
Lohmann components	Ts	Ls	Circular	Courtyards	Post wall buildings	Varney	Yankee-town	Celt	Shell bead	Thread	References
Cahokia ICT-II, 15A-DT	x	x	x	?		x	x	x	x	x	Collins 1990; Pauketat 1998a, 1998b
Hal Smith					x						Notes on file (University of Illinois Urbana-Champaign)
Knoebel		x		x			x	x		x	Alt 2002b; Bareis 1976; Holley, Parker, Watters, Harper, Skele, Ringberg, Brown, and Booth 2001; Kruchten 2012
Pfeffer	x		x		x		x	x	x		Notes on file (University of Illinois Urbana-Champaign)
Halliday	x			X	x	x	x			x	Alt 2001, 2002a; notes on file (University of Illinois Urbana-Champaign)

production that ranged from shell-bead and celt manufacture to the production of cordage for textiles. Pottery manufacture might have been less restricted, and ceramic assemblages in the uplands were characterized by more or less Cahokian appearances. The most aberrant vessel assemblage was connected with Halliday, where the Varney Red Filmed vessels were common and where shell temper was more common than at Cahokia.

The adoption of wall trenches also occurred very differently in the uplands. The inhabitants of the upland settlements appear to have responded differently in the face of this new manner of building homes. Halliday residents maintained single-post construction techniques until the early Stirling phase, and only some hybrid or faux wall trenches were apparent before 1100. So, too, some of the buildings at Pfeffer and Hal Smith were built using single-set posts, while others were constructed with wall trenches, perhaps indicating that the intermittent occupation involved people from divergent backgrounds. In contrast, the families of Knoebel began the Lohmann phase by quickly adopting wall-trench structures (Alt 2002b).

From this architectural evidence, it appears that most upland inhabitants were aware of the new Cahokian construction styles. Some experimented with different house construction technologies. Some, at Knoebel, readily altered their home-building practices, but they did not change the location or orientation of their homes, in contrast with people living in downtown Cahokia and the floodplain. And yet three of the four settlements reviewed here contained one or more buildings that Emerson (1997a, 1997b) described as Cahokia's "architecture of power." Of course, the numbers and types of these constructions vary among the four reviewed sites, with single T-shaped buildings known only from Pfeffer and Halliday, and a lone circular building found only at Pfeffer. Knoebel's L-shaped buildings may or may not be comparable to those known from Cahokia and its vicinity. Certainly its courtyard organization, similar to that at Halliday, was more characteristic of Terminal Late Woodland village life than it was of Cahokian order.

Overall, there is something like an urban/hinterland dichotomy between the settlements of the floodplain and those of the uplands. The floodplain inhabitants were more homogeneous in their everyday lives and stylistic trappings, if more diverse in their economic and political practices. Upland people, by contrast, were diverse culturally but not economically. They lived in modest villages with less social differentiation. In general, settlements located on the American Bottom floodplain, including those summarized in Chapter 2, were more similar to the neighborhoods of downtown Cahokia than were the Richland Complex settlements. The Richland people retained characteristics of some pre-Mississippian organizational and technological practices. That is, each of the upland villages is similar to Cahokia in some ways and strikingly dissimilar in other ways. No two village trajectories seem alike, doubtless a result in part of each inhabitant's or group's different history prior to their relocation as part of the Richland Complex. But their experiences in place remain to be explored. Did the Richland farmers influence or affect Cahokians? If so, how?

A fifth upland site, Grossmann, excavated in its entirety, provides answers to these questions. I turn next to that site and its architectural and material remains.

4
The Architecture of Grossmann

The Grossmann site is located 16 km southeast of Cahokia on a prominent upland ridge that divides the drainages of Richland and Silver Creeks, 2.5 and 6 km away, respectively (see Figure 3.1). It was founded in the midst of numerous Richland Complex settlements large and small, including the four contemporary settlements reviewed in the previous chapter. Halliday and Hal Smith sit just 1.5 and 4 km to the north-northwest, respectively. Knoebel is located 6 km to the east-southeast; Pfeffer is located 8 km to northeast. Many other unexcavated sites, likely dating to the same period, are known in this portion of the Richland Complex, including the previously mentioned Lehman-Somers site (4 km southwest) and another large and poorly understood village, the Miller Farm site, 9.5 km due south (Wilson 1998). A series of more than a half dozen farmsteads or field house sites surround Grossmann (Pauketat et al. 2002).

Background and Site Organization

The Grossmann site was identified during a pedestrian survey in 1997 that was part of a new roadway mitigation project conducted by the Illinois Transportation Archaeological Research Program (ITARP) (Jackson 2000). ITARP activities included a controlled surface collection of the entire site surface, followed in 1998 by excavations of 20 structures and 37 pits in the southern portion of the site in a proposed road right-of-way. Under my direction in 2001 and 2002, the University of Illinois's Richland Archaeological Project (RAP) conducted an additional pedestrian survey of the locality, geophysical investigations of Grossmann itself, and

Figure 4.1. Excavations at the Grossmann site, 2001, showing mechanical stripping of western edge of site.

Figure. 4.2. Excavations at the Grossmann site, 2001, showing building basins under excavation, view to southwest.

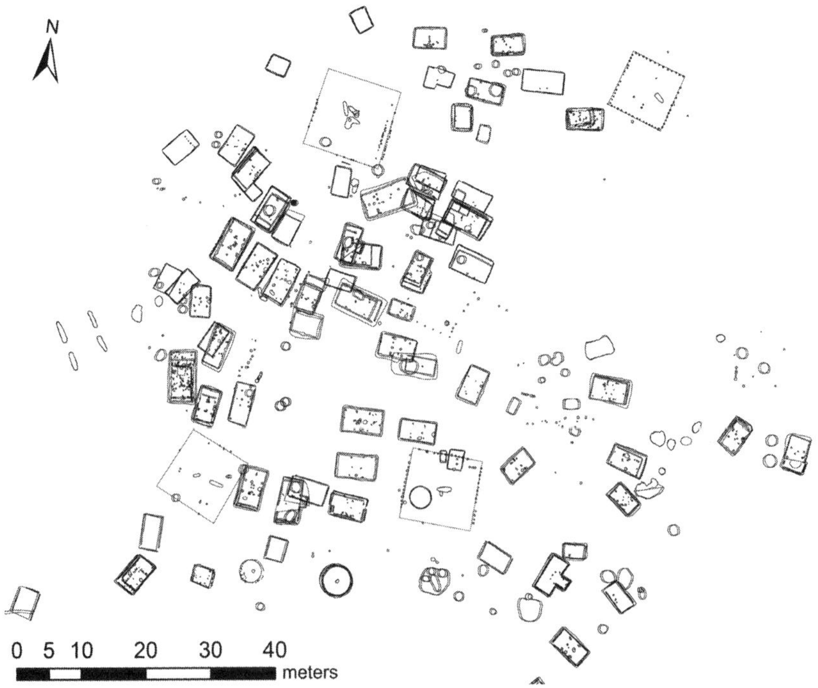

Figure 4.3. Plan view of the Grossmann site: 1998, 2001, and 2002 excavations.

excavations of the remaining portions of the site (Hargrave et al. 2002). The ITARP materials were integrated with the RAP project and are the basis of my present analysis (Evans 2005; Jackson 2004). Over the course of the three field seasons, heavy machinery was used to clear the plow zone of an area of approximately 2.3 ha (including a buffer of up to 25 m extending beyond the limits of identified features) as well as to locate and excavate an additional 93 structures and 58 pits (Figures 4.1 and 4.2).

In addition to the 113 structures and 95 pits, there were also 10 post pits and 4 truss trenches, the latter being likely foundations for a single elevated wooden platform (Wittry et al. 1994). There were also 6 short fences or screens, 31 isolated posts, and 10 discrete middens. Of course, not all features were used concurrently. With the aid of diagnostic attributes of pottery, features were seriated into three phases: late Lohmann, early Stirling, and middle Stirling (Holley 1989; Jackson and Finney 2007; Jackson et al. 1992; Pauketat 1998a). A total of 106 features could be sorted into these three divisions: 39 features to the late Lohmann phase, 29 to the early Stirling phase, and 38 to the middle Stirling phase (Figure 4.3). Two radio-

Table 4.1. Grossmann Radiocarbon Assays

Feature	% Area enclosed	Cal A.D. age range	Relative area under probability distribution
Feature 256	68.3 (1 sigma)	1023–1036	0.876
		1144–1147	0.124
	95.4 (2 sigma)	1020–1040	0.683
		1099–1117	0.124
		1141–1152	0.193
Feature 275	68.3 (1 sigma)	985–1068	0.574
		1081–1125	0.282
	95.4 (2 sigma)	1136–1158	0.144
		897– 922	0.041
		942–1212	0.959

Note: Calibration calculated using CALIB REV 4.4.2.

carbon dates from burned thatch in two features at Grossmann confirmed the placement of the Grossmann sequence vis-à-vis the overall regional chronology (Table 4.1).

In general, the Lohmann phase is identifiable through ceramic characteristics such as a high incidence of shell temper, somewhat angular vessel shoulders, and smooth vessel exteriors that are often slipped, with red slip most common. Lohmann phase vessels are more angular and have shorter necks than Terminal Late Woodland pottery, but they are not as angular or as short necked as Stirling phase pottery. The subsequent Stirling phase is further identifiable through horizon markers such as Ramey Incised pottery. Such characteristics make it possible to seriate within the Stirling phase, as well as to distinguish between the Lohmann and Stirling phases.

All things considered, the duration of the Grossmann site occupation is unlikely to have exceeded 50 years, with the site founded up to three or four decades after other Richland sites. Specifically, there were no Edelhardt (A.D. 1000–1050), early Lohmann (A.D. 1050–1075), or late Stirling phase (A.D. 1150–1200) ceramics at the site, suggesting a founding date after A.D. 1075 and an abandonment date before A.D. 1150. Moreover, there was a maximum of three rebuilding episodes of any given pole-and-thatch structure, which, given reasonable use-life estimates of around 15 years for these buildings (Pauketat 2003), means a circa 45-year use life for the entire complex. Presumably, no more than a third of the buildings, fewer than 40, were standing at any one time.

Unlike the inhabitants of the nearby farming villages, Grossmann's inhabitants often rebuilt structures using the same footprint of previous buildings, a use of space comparable to that seen in Cahokian residential areas but only rarely in the Richland Complex contexts discussed so far. At Cahokia, multiple rebuildings in the same location have been taken to indicate that usable building space was at a premium (Dalan et al. 2003; Milner 1998). However, at Grossmann, space was available. In fact, there were large, flat, open spaces at the same elevations and atop the very same soils where no structures were ever built. Because there was no microenvironmental rationale for rebuilding patterns, it is likely that particular organizational rules or sensibilities dictated where structures and open areas could and should be located. In addition, some buildings may have been connected to the status, identity, or occupational specialization of the resident. These kinds of rules for spatial organizational have been noted for historical Native American settlements across North America, and the organization of Cahokian settlements in particular has been described as rigidly ordered (Collins 1997; Mehrer and Collins 1995; Smith 1969).

Late Lohmann phase features were more densely located in the southern and southeastern site area, while early Stirling phase structures were more common north of that area, and middle Stirling phase buildings were clearly more densely packed and restricted in the central area of the site. There were always densely packed structures in this core area of the complex. Public structures, however, were not located in this central block and were not rebuilt in place.

Structures

The Grossmann site's 113 buildings range in size from miniature, as in a mortuary building with an internal floor area of only 1.4 m^2, to public, as in the largest of four square buildings with a floor area of 120 m^2. Nearly all structures (93 percent) were built with wall-trench construction, with the notable exception of the public buildings and four other likely nondomestic buildings: one circular sweat lodge, two storage structures, and a small rectangular building.

A total of 39 hearths were found on the floors of 17 rectangular and 2 circular structures, which contrasts with the lower frequency at other domestic sites in the region (Collins 1990; Milner et al. 1984). Several build-

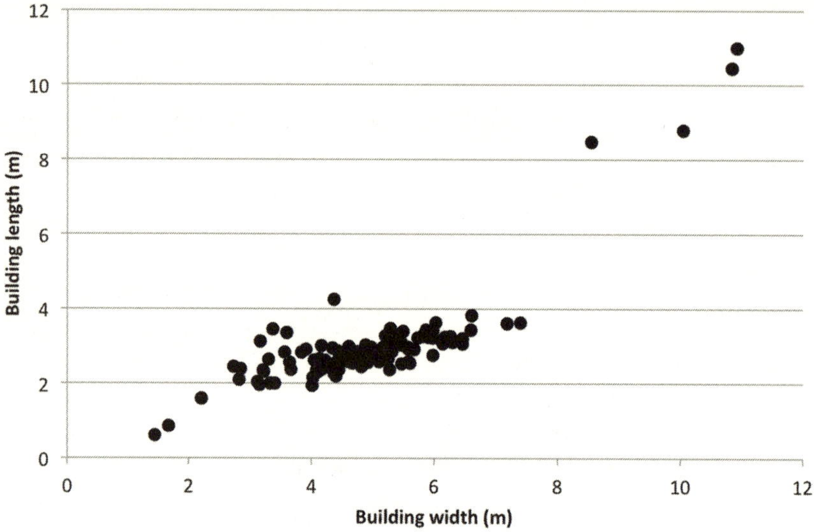

Figure 4.4. Building sizes, Grossmann site.

ings had more than one hearth, each little more than a small burned spot on the structure's floor. A few more contained formally prepared, deep-set basin hearths, including one in a circular building (F9), likely a sweat lodge.

With an overall average floor area of 17 m^2, Grossmann buildings fall at the large end of the building size range in the region. Forty (35 percent) of the Grossmann buildings were smaller than the average Richland Complex building, and 16 (14 percent) were larger than the average for Tract 15A, the architectural dataset with the highest average building sizes. Cahokia's Tract 15A was covered in buildings with a greater average floor area, an average skewed by that tract's extraordinarily large public buildings (Pauketat 1998a).

Unusually large structures also have an effect on Grossmann's building size averages (Figure 4.4), making the average Grossmann structure larger than the typical building at similarly dated sites in the region outside Cahokia proper. The larger building sizes at Grossmann were not single-family domiciles. Building shapes and architectural styles bolster this interpretation. In fact, the four largest structures were square in plan view and were built using single-set posts. Others were T-shaped, L-shaped, and circular. These are all typical of the "architecture of power" of Cahokia's Lohmann and Stirling phase buildings, but the entire set is uncommon at outlying domestic sites. What were they and what are the implications of the suite at Grossmann?

Public Structures

Four structures at Grossmann (F151/152, F216, F248, and F249) were unusually large (Figure 4.5). Their floor areas ranged from 72 to 120 m^2 (mean 98.5 m^2), while the average floor space for all Grossmann structures was a much smaller 18 m^2. These large structures were nearly square and, unlike the Grossmann norm, were built using single-set wall-post construction, with large posts that averaged 20 cm in diameter (compared to the typical post-mold diameters for Grossmann buildings of 7 to 14 cm). I suspect that the four buildings were built one at a time, such that at least one would have been standing at any given time during the history of the complex. This is supported by the superimposition of F216 by two later wall-trench structures if not also a circular building (it might have superimposed that building instead).

Possibly, the single-set post walls of these buildings harked back to more traditional construction methods, providing a more traditional feel while simultaneously introducing new political and social relationships. In any case, these large single-set wall posts were relatively shallow, with an average depth of only 13 cm. Of course, the upper 25 cm of the potential post depth was lost to the modern plowing of the site, which churned up the site surface. Both facts indicate that these large buildings were probably built on the surface, lacking the typical semisubterranean basin of other structures, meaning that we lost some if not most of the posthole depth in the 25 cm of plow zone (removed prior to feature identification and excavation). Thus, if the house floor was at natural ground level, then the average depth of the posts would have been about 38 cm.

The roofs of these large buildings, with shallow or no basins, were supported by at least one sizable center post (see Figure 4.5). Some center posts were offset from the building center. In two cases, this may have been because of the periodic need to replace an earlier post owing to rot or renewal ceremonialism. Those two buildings had reset center posts (F148 and F151/152 had two post pits each). Another had a large section of a burned post still in place in the post ramp (Figure 4.6). A fourth had a noncarbonized sliver of wood, identified by Katie Parker as shortleaf pine (report on file, University of Illinois), in the base of the posthole. In each of six interior post pits, red ocher had been sprinkled into the soil used to backfill the insertion or extraction ramps. These posts were up to 1 m

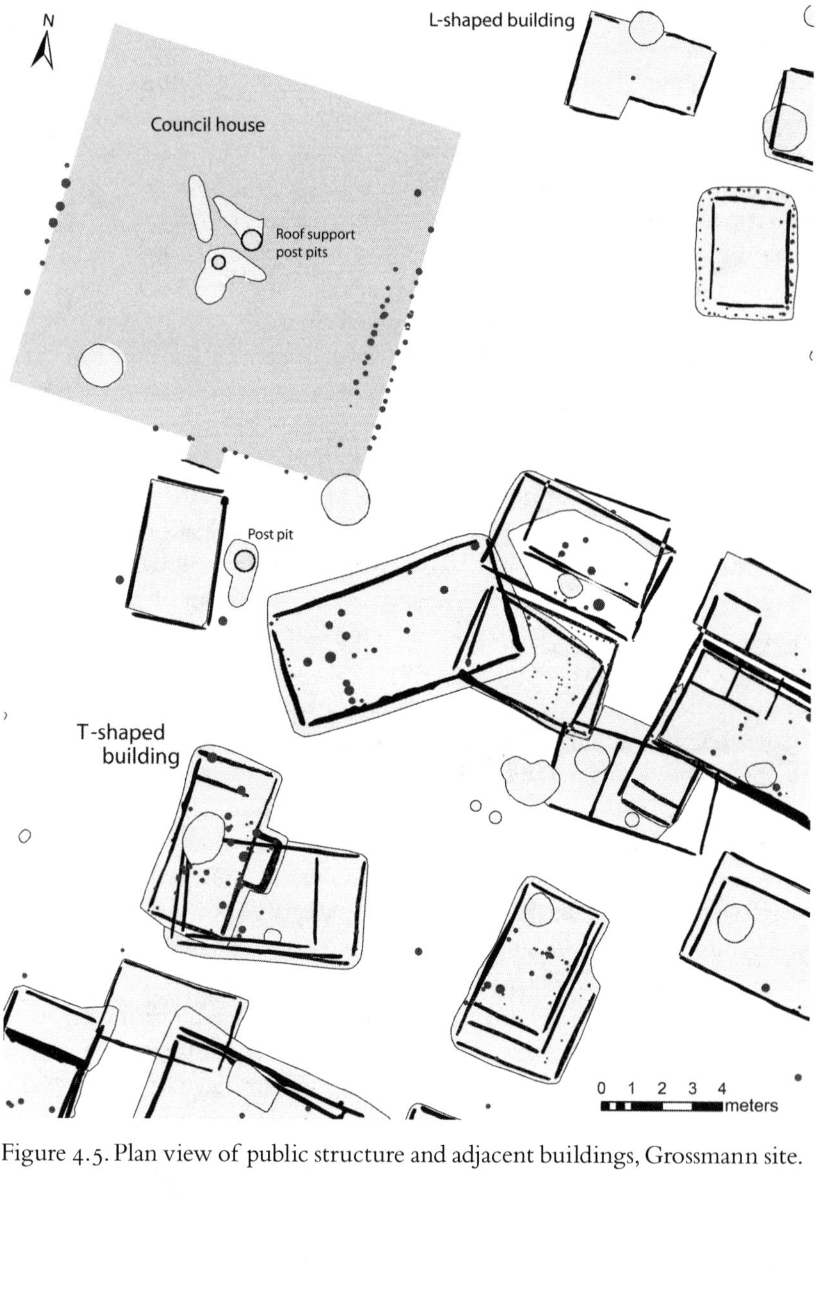

Figure 4.5. Plan view of public structure and adjacent buildings, Grossmann site.

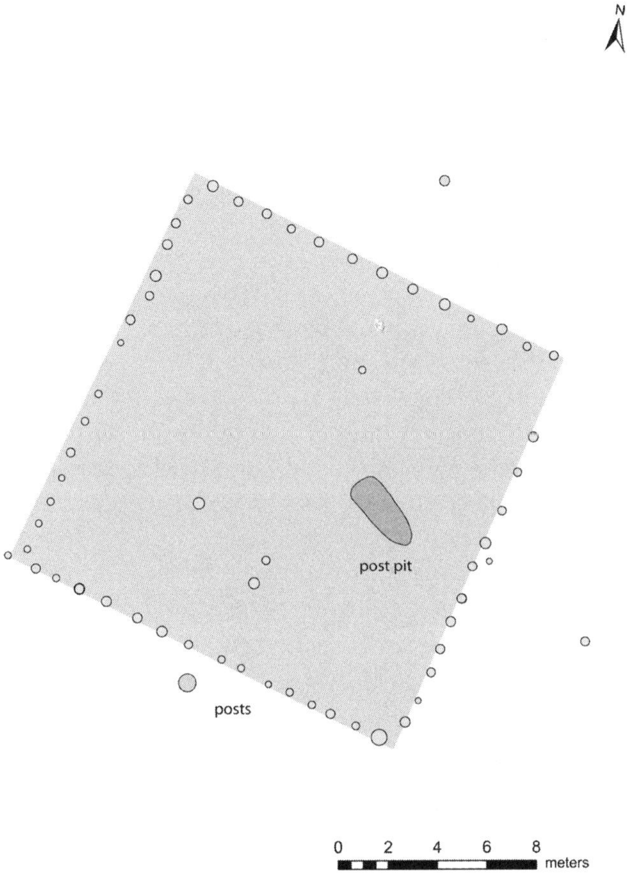

Figure 4.6. Plan view of public building, Grossmann site.

deep, ignoring the 25 cm plow zone. In diameter, the central support posts would have measured from 35 to 75 cm, meaning that they were capable of supporting massive roofs.

Other than an interior post or posts, these buildings had few internal features and little debris. Two Grossmann buildings (F248 and F151/152) did have small pits in their corners. But little to no debris was associated with them or with any of the interior or wall posts. As collected and mapped by ITARP personnel prior to excavation, little surface debris was found in any public-building location. Hence, these buildings appear to have been kept clean, and I infer that their cleanliness marks them as public constructions.

Buildings of similar size and shape and with similar construction details have been reported at Cahokia, East St. Louis, Mitchell, and smaller floodplain sites (Hanenberger 2003; Pauketat 1998a, 2005b; Porter 1974). At Cahokia, one such Stirling phase building, but with wall-trench construction, occupied the center of the Woodhenge space. At Mitchell, they were found beneath mounds. At the Range "nodal" site, a large single-post structure dating to the Lohmann or Stirling phase had little or no basin and measured 7.6 × 7.6 m (57.8 m^2 of floor space); it also had large, widely spaced wall posts, pits in the corners, and a central post pit nearly 1 m deep.

The Lohmann phase Range site structure is interpreted as a "community building," analogous to the town houses known for Historic Creek (Hanenberger 2003:63). This interpretation seems compatible with the Grossmann buildings, which were structurally very different from any other building on the site. It is reasonable to suppose that they and their locations on the outer edges of the village were extraordinary. The large wall posts suggest the creation of a sizable gathering space in a building intended to last (Rapoport 1982, 1990).

Very large buildings, particularly those associated with mounds, are sometimes called temples, with the term signifying a building dedicated primarily to religious purposes. It is possible that the Grossmann buildings were temples. However, ethnohistorical descriptions of southeastern "temples" do not match the particulars of the buildings excavated at Grossmann (DePratter 1983; Knight 1986). For the most part, southeastern temples were mortuary facilities. These were places where the bones of ancestors—the remains of past leaders—were curated alongside other important religious objects—valued goods and effigies (Hudson 1976; Swanton 1979). Members of the de Soto party looted a temple at Cofitachique, finding and stealing large amounts of pearls among the baskets of ancestral bones. The looting episode was recounted as follows: "He opened a temple that was there, where the important people of that land were buried, and we gathered from there a quantity of pearls; there must have been up to six and a half or seven arrobas of them, although they were not good because they were damaged through being below ground and placed amidst the adipose tissues of the Indians. Here we found buried two Castilian axes for cutting wood, and a rosary of beads of jet and some margaritas [i.e., trade beads] of the kind that they carry from here (Spain) to barter with the Indians" (Clayton et al. 1993:230–231).

In the American Bottom region, buildings associated with mounds but not containing human remains have also been considered temples. For example, structures associated with the Kunnemann mound were interpreted as temples (Pauketat 1993). The buildings found on or under mounds that are described as temples are large and, as importantly, are sometimes marked by specially prepared, plastered, or painted floors and formal hearths. The plastered Pfeffer site buildings might fit such a description (see Chapter 3), but Grossmann's public buildings do not.

They do fit the definition of council houses, and similar buildings have been identified archaeologically in the Cahokia region dating to as early as A.D. 600 (Kelly et al. 1990). In the Southeast, such constructions continued into the historic period. There are numerous accounts of such meetinghouses in early-contact literature (Adair 1930; Waselkov and Braund 1995). Some Creek examples were circular. Cherokee town houses were described as sugarloaf shaped (Swanton 1979:402). As Adair noted, "Every town has a large edifice, which properly may be called the mountain house, in comparison with those already described. But the only difference between it and the winter house or stove, is in its dimensions, and application" (1930:453).

We cannot be certain that Cahokians had more buildings dedicated to special purposes than did other pre-Columbian North American peoples, but we can be certain that Cahokians did construct a greater diversity of building forms than anyone else. Given this, it would seem reasonable to posit that meetinghouses were among them. The evidence presented later in the book, in fact, suggests that Grossmann was a thirdspace where community and extracommunity people and things met. Such meetings are further revealed in other forms of architecture.

Sweat Lodges

Three of the structures at Grossmann were circular and relatively small (Figure 4.7). In the Cahokia region, small circular buildings are most commonly interpreted as sweat lodges (Emerson 1997a; Mehrer 1995). This identification is based on ethnographic analogy as well as on the presence of deep interior hearths that occasionally contain burned rocks (Collins 1990; Emerson 1997a; Pauketat 1998a). For example, at the Range site, circular structures had evidence of deep, intensely fired central hearths and limestone-paved floors. The Range structures also had multiple rows of posts, which may represent bench supports along the interior walls (Hanenberger 2003).

Sweat lodges were widely known in North American societies, and a variety of regional construction styles and uses have been reported (Bucko 1998; Faulkner 1977; Lopatin 1960; Mehta 2007). In some places, sweathouses or sweat lodges were said to be places for healing and purification. As reported by Swanton (1979:785), the Indians of Virginia used sweat

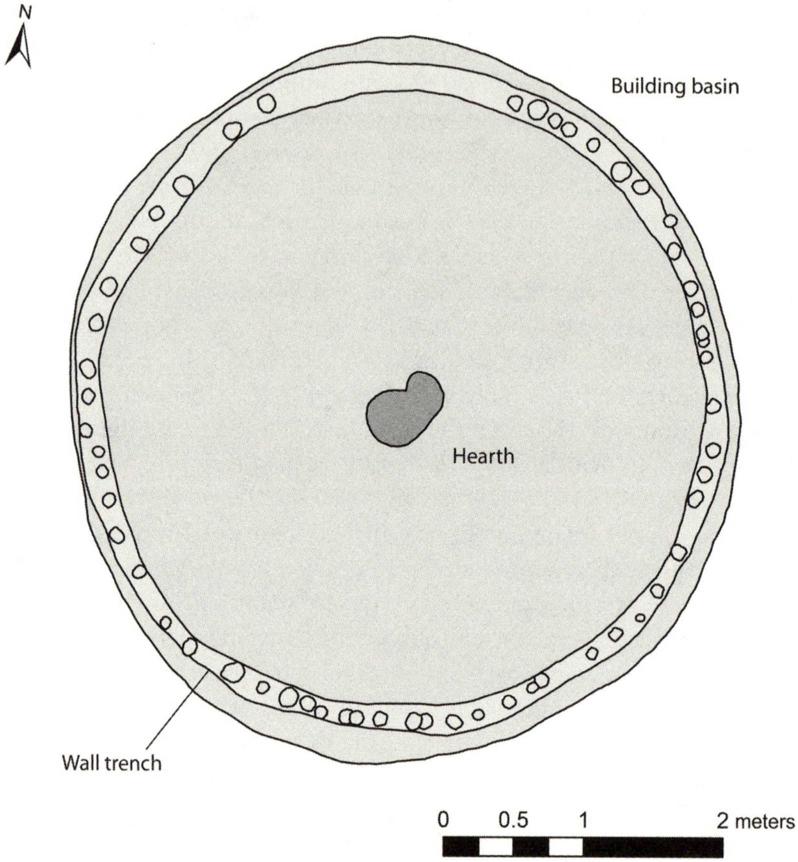

Figure 4.7. Plan view of circular sweat lodge, Grossmann site.

baths to "refresh themselves after they have been fatigued with hunting travel or the like or when they are troubled with agues, aches or pains in their limbs." Sweat baths were also used to cure illnesses and to overcome pollution (Hudson 1976:345; Swanton 1979:790–791). That is, from the northern plains to the Southeast, circular sweat lodges were used for purification (Ehrlich 1937; Hudson 1976). In some places and times, sweat lodges were temporary constructions intended for a specific use (Grinnell 1919; Murie 1981). In other places, they assumed more central ritual roles (Bucko 1998).

It is assumed that Mississippian sweat lodges relate to an emphasis on purification as part of religious practices (Emerson 1997a). All three of the Grossmann circular structures were located at the southern end of the settlement. They were small, with mean diameters of 3.6 m and floor areas that averaged 10.5 m^2, as typical in the region (Mehrer 1995). Two of them had hearths in their centers (F9 and F20), while the third (F215) did not have a basin or a hearth and was probably disturbed by plowing. It is also possible that one of the meetinghouses (F216) was constructed on top of it.

Both F9 and F215 lacked basins and material remains in posts and wall trenches. A small fired-clay animal effigy was found in F20. The F9 building had single-post walls, while the F20 and F215 lodges were built using wall trenches. Given that all buildings at the site were rebuilt three times, it could be that construction of the sweat lodges was sequential, and one building was used until it needed replacement. It is therefore possible that F9 was earliest, and the others later.

T-Shaped Structures

T-shaped structures are a variation on the standard rectangular buildings of the Lohmann and Stirling phases. The T structures at Grossmann varied in construction details and size, with floor areas of 14.9, 17.27, and 24.3 m^2. Beyond size differences, the T structures seem to reveal particulars about the site's history (Figures 4.8 and 4.9).

First, there would have been a T structure in use at any given time at the site, as the three T-shaped structures seriated into each of the site's phases. The earlier two structures were larger, as well as more peripherally located in relation to the other buildings. The later Stirling phase T structure was more centrally located and flanked with two other much larger structures (F148 and F198—both of these flanking buildings contained a high density of exotic material). F47 was the earliest and largest of the T structures, dating to the late Lohmann phase. The wall trenches of this feature contained multiple individual posts in the trenches, and its T alcove had double walls. An arc of posts inside the building appears to have been for a wall or screen that would have separated the alcove from the main area of the building. This structure was also on the southern side of the site but was located farther east than its successor, F6.

F6 dates to the early Stirling phase and was located near the three sweat lodges on the southern side of the site. Several small hearths or burned areas were located on the F6 floor in front of the T alcove as well as two lines of wall trenches on the northern and southern walls that appear to relate to interior benches. On the F6 floor were also two large storage pits, the fills of which postdate the structure itself, suggesting that they remained open after the building was dismantled or that they had been intentionally emplaced within the footprint of the abandoned but still-

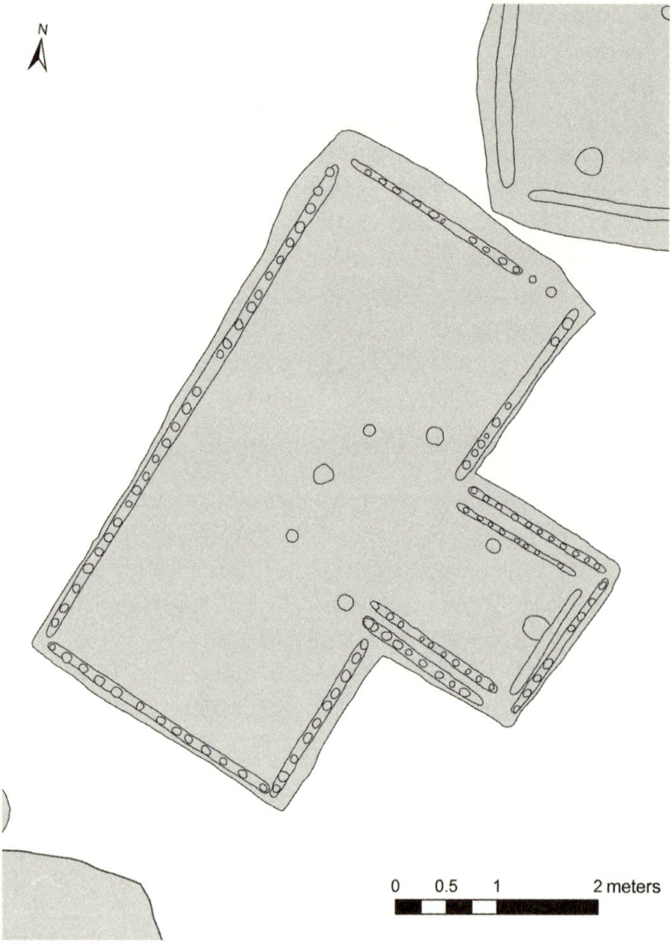

Figure 4.8. Plan view of T-shaped building, Grossmann site.

remembered T structure location. Most notable among the F6 pits was one (F220) containing a human burial. The articulated skeleton of an adult woman in flexed position was found at the base of this deep bell-shaped pit (Eve Hargrave, notes on file, University of Illinois). Imprints in the soil indicate that the woman appeared to have been wrapped in a woven material prior to burial. An offering had been burned on her chest, and a broken celt was placed under her arm.

F166 was the smallest and latest of the T-shaped structures, dating to the middle Stirling phase. Like F6, it had been built over another structure and contained a large storage pit (but no burial). Unlike the two preced-

Figure 4.9. Oblique photograph of building floor, Grossmann site.

ing buildings, this T structure was located in the complex's center, where it was surrounded (protected?) by other buildings. The T alcove here also had a double wall, and there is evidence of a bench on the north side of the structure. There is some suggestion that F166 may have been ritually terminated or closed. There was evidence of burning on the northeast side of the structure where some posts had actually burned down into the ground. As this special structure was standing when the site was being abandoned, it may have been necessary to incinerate rather than simply abandon it. The spatial arrangement of nearby buildings F166, F198, and F148 suggests that they may have been linked to this T structure.

Similar T-shaped buildings are known from Cahokia as well as from outlying "nodal" or religious sites, but they are by no means common (see Chapters 2 and 3). In part because of its rare occurrence, the T building has been assumed to be a special-function building. The identification of T-shaped buildings on the summits of mounds and lining plazas at Cahokia has certainly bolstered arguments for these buildings being associated with special uses (Collins 1990; Pauketat 1993, 1998a, 2013a). T-shaped buildings were found atop Mounds 11 and 50 at Cahokia and in association with a mound at the Mitchell site (Gergen and Iseminger 1987; Pauketat 1993; Porter 1974). Even when not associated with mounds, T-shaped buildings seem to be otherwise marked as unusual. Two T-shaped structures identified at Cahokia's Tract 15A were located in building clusters associated with sweat lodges, while a third, much larger than the two mentioned, was located on the edge of a Tract 15A plaza (Pauketat 1998b). A T-shaped structure found at ICT-II was located in a cluster of Lohmann phase structures encircled by four features oriented to cardinal directions, a pattern thought to be a cosmic reference (Collins 1990:81).

Given the association of the T-shaped structures and mounds, I believe it is likely that the buildings were the domiciles of leaders with religious powers, something similar to what has been discussed in the literature as chiefs' or religious leaders' houses (see also Collins 1990). Features of leaders' houses are compatible with the Mississippian T-shaped structure:

> The difference between the houses of the lords or principal men and the others is that besides being larger they have large balconies in front and below seats resembling benches made of canes; and round about many barbacoas in which they gather the tribute paid to them by their Indians which consists of maize and deerskins and native blankets resembling shawls, some being made of the inner bark of the trees and some from a plant like daffodils which when pounded remains like flax (Swanton 1979:387).

> As the Jews had a sanctum sanctorum, or most holy place, so have all of the Indian nations; particularly, the Muskogee. It is partitioned off by a mud-wall about breast high, behind the white seat which always stands to the left hand of the red painted war seat; there they deposit their consecrated vessels, and supposedly holy utensils, none of the laity daring to approach that sacred place, for fear of particular damage to themselves, and general hurt to the people from the supposed divinity of the place (Adair 1930:84).

Houses with balconies in front, or walled-off inner sanctums, can be imagined to have created something like the Cahokian T-shaped wall patterns we find archaeologically. The Swanton quotation adds an expectation for nearby storage facilities, while the Adair quotation suggests that a chief's structure would also contain special goods; perhaps this would be where objects such as a sacred bundle would be kept (Pauketat et al. 2012). But this may also then indicate that the T building was a place for priests associated with a leader's compound. This interpretation actually better fits the evidence at Grossmann.

Claudine Payne (1994) conducted a study of Mississippian capitals and determined that chiefs' houses were usually on mounds and were larger and more "expensive" than commoners' houses. Her sense of expensive refers to investment in building materials, better overall construction, and more decoration on the exterior as well as the interior walls. A chief's house might be plastered even when a commoner's house was not. Chiefs' houses might also be decorated with wall paintings and matting, and they were associated with more and larger storage facilities than commoners' houses. Finally, Payne found that chiefs' houses were generally similar in shape to commoners' houses but with an added portico.

Importantly, although previously suspected to be porticos and entrances, the T alcoves on the Grossmann and Cahokian buildings were demonstrably not entryways. Instead, the building entrances were on the wall directly opposite the T alcove (Porter 1974). The alcove, then, was a room for keeping powerful, likely religious, objects away from those who did not have the powers or training to be able to see or handle such things. In ethnohistorical reports, some families had a responsibility to curate and manage objects of great cultural importance, and this responsibility was bestowed on a particular person spiritually chosen to be appropriate for the task. In other cases, a leader might be the holder of an entire people's sacred bundle. At Grossmann, all lines of evidence—adjacent buildings, hearths on the floors, and materials found in and near these basins (galena, hematite, and special-use pottery)—suggest that the T-shaped structures were occupied by persons with special powers or responsibilities.

Storage and L-Shaped Buildings

The T alcoves were a kind of special or sacred storage, but more basic food-storage needs were met by other buildings at Grossmann. Of course, large subterranean pits were used for long-term food storage, especially at ordinary domestic sites where pits are usually common. At Grossmann, storage pits are relatively uncommon, if voluminous (Figure 4.10). Indeed, comparisons with Collins's (1990:221–222) numbers show that Grossmann had little pit storage potential (Figure 4.11). Clearly, there were other forms of storage in use, and storage buildings are evident at the site, if indicative of shorter-term storage.

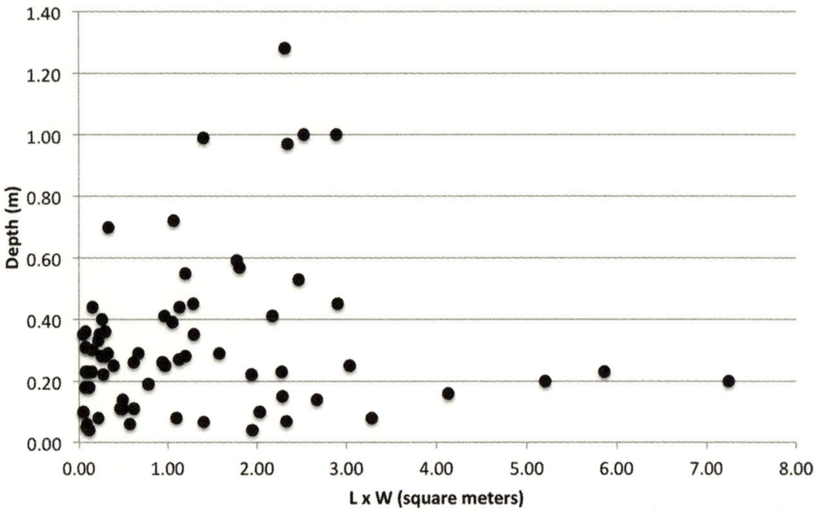

Figure 4.10. Scatter plot of pit sizes at Grossmann.

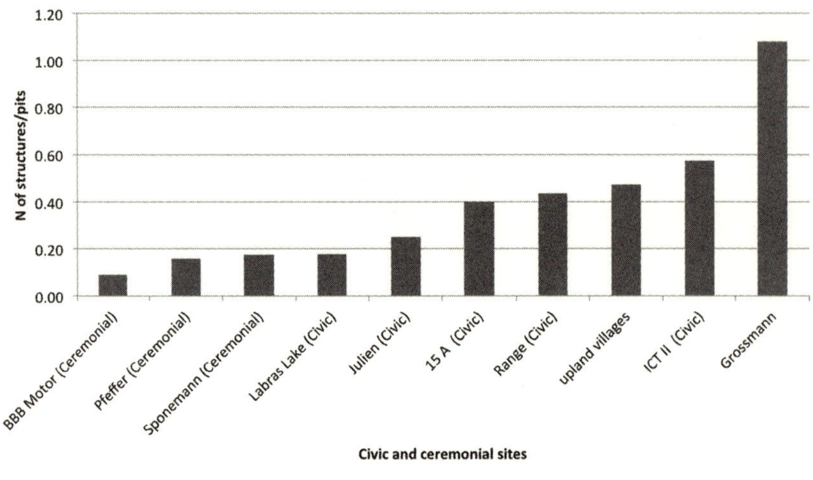

Figure 4.11. Bar chart showing structure-pit index among select sites.

Elsewhere in the Mississippian Southeast, pit storage was also less common than might be expected. At some Mississippian sites, storage was typically in structures, located either in a corner of a residential house or in a separate building (Barrier 2011; Blitz 1993; DeBoer 1988; Hally 1986; Welch and Scarry 1995). According to ethnohistorical records, the separate storage structures were often in the form of corncribs (Payne 1994; Welch and Scarry 1995). Swanton notes that "they have barbacoas in which they keep their maize. This is a house raised up on four posts, timbered like a loft and the floor of canes" (Swanton 1979:378). Following such ethnohistorical reports, John Blitz (1993) used the lack of floor staining as well as the presence of burned corn kernels and daub to identify possible storage houses at the Mississippian Lubbub Creek site in Alabama.

In the American Bottom region, small, square buildings—perhaps analogous to corncribs—have been identified as storage structures (Alt 2002b; Collins 1990; Pauketat 2005). Before accepting that interpretation for the Grossmann buildings, I investigated the possibility that these unusual small buildings were menstrual huts by comparing data at Grossmann with ethnohistorical reports of Cherokee menstrual huts (some of the only such data available), but there is a complete lack of supporting evidence for such an interpretation. The floors do not show use-wear evidence that might be expected if the women of a family group were spending three to five days a month living in these buildings. They also do not have hearths or other interior features that would suggest occupation. Other lines of evidence for menstrual huts such as nearness to water and serving dishes are also lacking. It should be kept in mind that it is possible that in the American Bottom there are no menstrual huts to find. While groups such as the Cherokee did practice menstrual segregation, not all Native American societies, for example, Plains groups such as the Crow, followed this practice. This may speak to differences in women's perceived roles and powers in different regions and/or times and may be a useful clue in tracking Cahokian descendants.

At Grossmann, the smaller square buildings were often clustered around the larger structures (see Figure 4.5). As measured with an index created by dividing house width by length, 22 of the Grossmann structures were more square than the more typically rectangular form seen for Lohmann and Stirling phase structures at American Bottom sites. These structures vary in construction details and deposition patterns, but then so do buildings confidently identified as storage structures at other sites. Some of these features, such as F228, F277, F145, F199, and F11, fit all expectations for storage structures, including location near larger structures, square shape, and lack of internal features or floor staining (Figure 4.12).

There may be another type of storage structure at Grossmann, the L-shaped building. The earliest reported appearance of L-shaped structures in the American Bottom region was during the Terminal Late Woodland period, though whether the buildings identified were actual L-shaped constructions or superimposed rectangular buildings remains an open ques-

Figure 4.12. Floor of a storage building, Grossmann site.

tion (Fortier 1996; Milner 1984a. Lohmann and Stirling phase L-shaped buildings are reported from Cahokia and its immediate vicinity and nodal settlements, including the distant Marty Coolidge site (Kuttruff 1972). Given their low occurrence at other sites, it has been suggested that L-shaped structures were special-function buildings, possibly with religious or political significance similar to T buildings (Collins 1990). But little material support for this interpretation exists, and the Knoebel buildings (Chapter 3) seem especially good candidates for domiciles with extra storage potential. Certainly, keeping stored goods attached to living quarters makes some sense, particularly if security was a concern.

There were at least two L-shaped structures at Grossmann (with a mean floor area of 20.3 m^2), and possibly two more (Figure 4.13). The latter (F188) was either an odd T-form building or a rebuilt L-shaped construction. All actual or possible L-shaped buildings at Grossmann lacked basins, perhaps conforming to expectations for storage facilities rather than living quarters. The L-shaped structures also lacked internal features and floor staining. Given that storage structures would not be subjected to the same kind of day-to-day movements of people as a domicile, storage structures should have fewer floor stains and floor depressions than houses.

Other rectangular structures at Grossmann have few to no interior features as well as no floor alteration. I suspect that these even larger rectangular structures may also have been used primarily for storage rather than

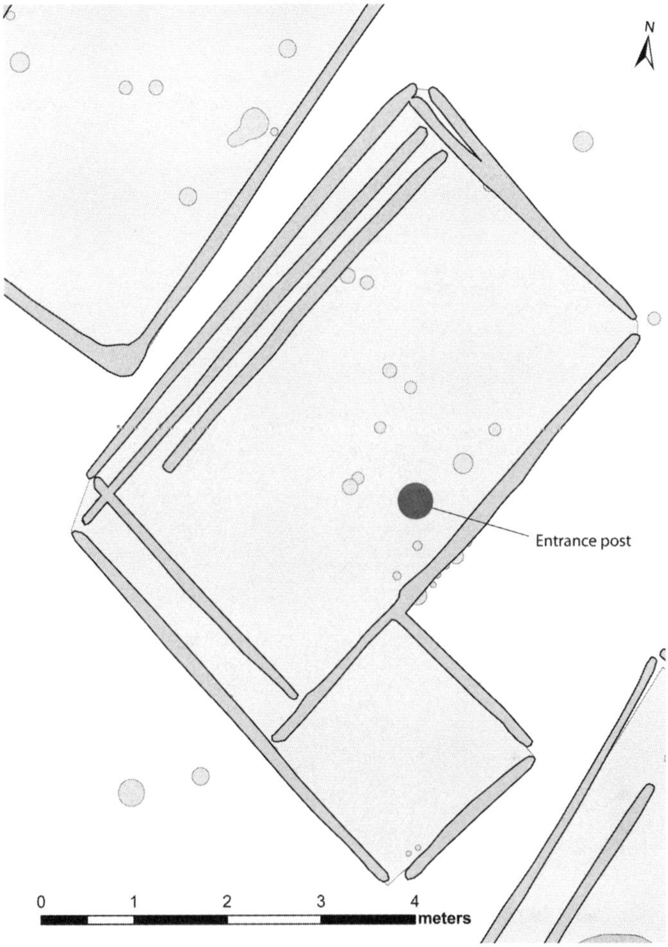

Figure 4.13. Plan view of L-shaped building, Grossmann site.

for housing. Indeed, if the assumption that building form predicts building use has any salience, the square and L shapes of some Grossmann structures suggest that at least 24 of the 113 structures at Grossmann could have been used for storage. That would mean that nearly one-fourth of the buildings at Grossmann were storage buildings. Other lines of evidence discussed later in this book suggest that this estimate is very likely correct.

Charnel House and Mortuary Platform

One Grossmann building fits ethnohistorical descriptions of a charnel house (Figure 4.14). This structure (F124) measured 1.68 × 0.86 m and

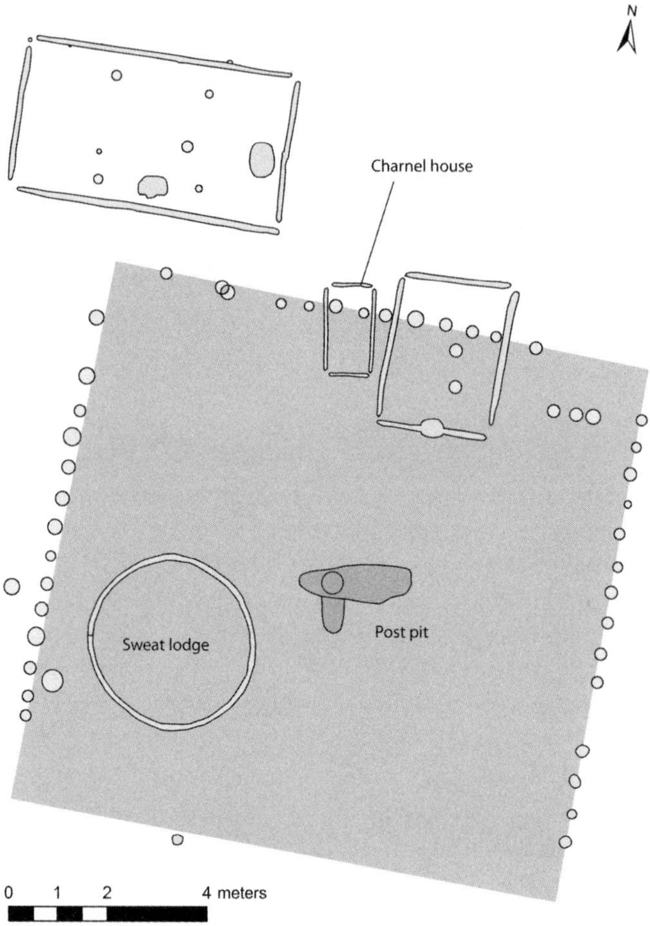

Figure 4.14. Plan view of charnel house, Grossmann site.

was possibly paired with another small structure (F125) that measured 2.8 × 2.1 m. Inside structure F124 were the remains of at least 18 people, which included adults, infants, and children, most represented by only a few skeletal elements (Otten 2011). The remains did not appear to have been carefully separated as discrete individuals but were placed as bundles of long bones and crania reminiscent of the "pile burials" interred in Mound 72 at Cahokia (Rose 1999). Many skeletal elements were missing, which may also indicate that remains were deposited in the building but later moved, perhaps to a nearby cemetery or back to Cahokia.

It is notable that buildings at other towns or centers have been interpreted as mortuaries or charnel houses, but other than the charnel house at the Lohmann site, this is the only such structure that contained human remains. Whether this building was meant to be a final resting place for the deceased or a temporary holding place is uncertain. If the latter, we might infer that the abandonment of Grossmann was not planned or that the remains in the building were overlooked or deemed unworthy of final burial.

In a review of ethnohistorical reports from between 1539 and 1730, Chester DePratter (1983) found that while size and shape varied, mortuary temples in the historical Southeast were usually located on mounds or near plazas. The temple entrances were always described as facing toward the east. The temples all possessed rooftop bird effigies that were also described as facing east (DePratter 1983:118–119). Inside, animal spirit effigies and human skulls were on display or were held in special receptacles, as were weapons, pearls, fabrics, matting, and baskets or wooden chests to hold the bodies and carved items such as statues. Some of the weapons described were European items obtained as a result of gifts, trade, or capture from the Spanish invaders. The association of statues or effigy figures and burial houses is consistent with archaeological evidence from the early Mississippian period.

At Grossmann, a carved and heat-exploded flint-clay smoking pipe depicting an owl was found across the plaza from the mortuary structure (see Chapter 5). Perhaps this is significant, since the association of mortuary temples and figurines is well known at the BBB Motor and Sponemann sites (see Chapter 2). Emerson's (1997a) descriptions point out how the Cahokian buildings diverge in other ways from the southeastern model. Around Cahokia, these were buildings where the dead might be processed for burial and perhaps temporarily stored. They were typically not intended to be the final resting place for the dead, with a prominent exception being the single-post building at Lohmann (Chapter 2). The evidence at Grossmann, that most individuals were represented by few elements, might argue that this building was like those at BBB Motor and Sponemann; that is, they were buildings used only for the preparation of the dead. In situations in which the dead were processed and then moved, it is unsurprising that there would be missing elements.

Placement in a charnel house was not the only evidence of mortuary activity at Grossmann. A few other individuals were buried in graves located within the complex, including an individual in a grave on the edge of a plaza and two other bodies, or parts of bodies, located in pits. All are unusual (Emerson and Hargrave 2000; Emerson et al. 2003). More impor-

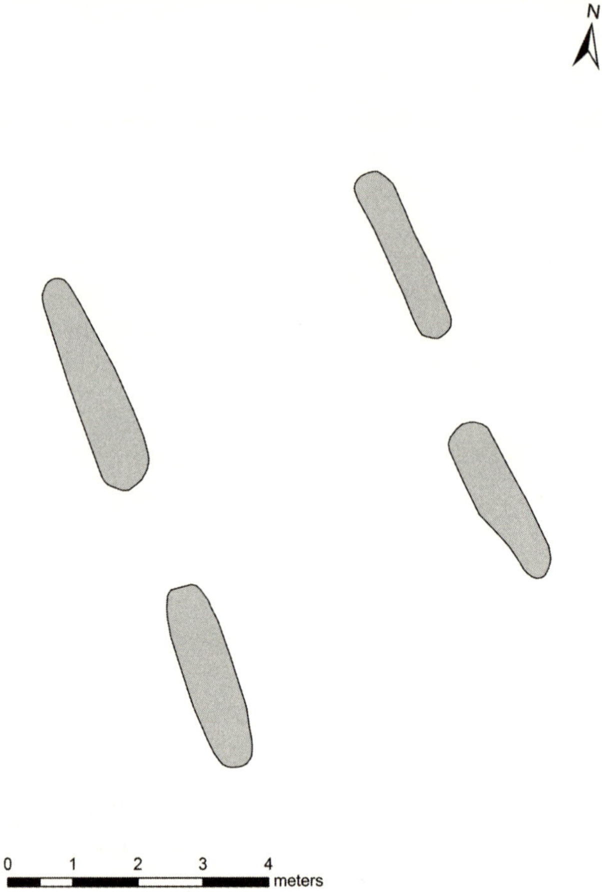

Figure 4.15. Plan view of truss trenches, foundations of a mortuary platform, Grossmann site.

tantly, perhaps, is the evidence of a large platform on the site's western edge, overlooking the Richland Creek valley beyond (Figure 4.15). This platform, similar to examples known from the nearby Knoebel locality, consisted of four truss trenches (Holley, Parker, Watters, Harper, Skele, Ringberg, et al. 2001). Warren Wittry argued years ago that the trenches at the Holdener site, also overlooking the American Bottom to the west, were the foundations for such mortuary platforms (Figure 4.16). The presumption is that bodies of the recent dead were placed atop the elevated platform, from which the bones would be retrieved weeks to months later. In the Holdener case, a mortuary building with single-set posts was also found in association with the truss trenches (Wittry et al. 1994).

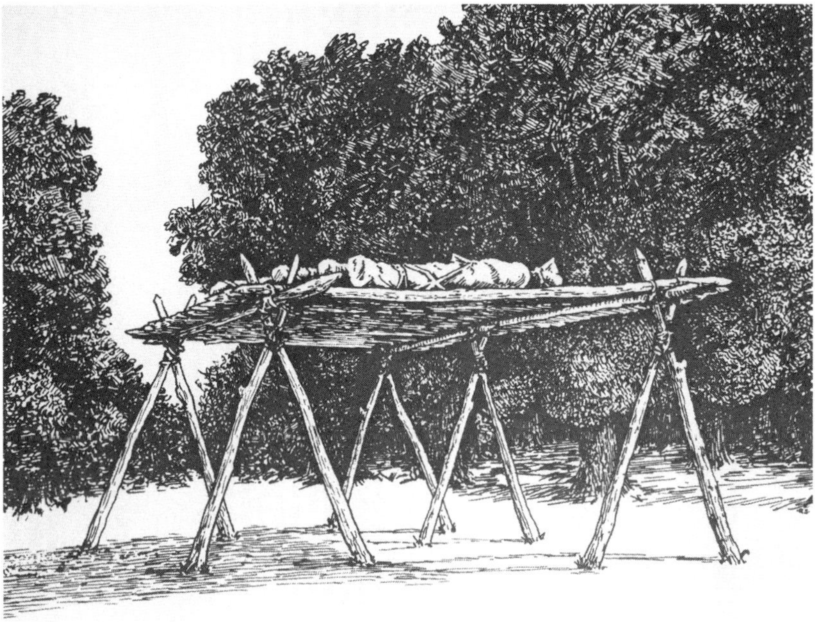

Figure 4.16. Artist's reconstruction of mortuary platform, Holdener site (from Wittry et al. 1994:Figure 14.8; courtesy of the Illinois State Archaeological Survey, University of Illinois).

At Grossmann, both the platform and charnel house may indicate that one of the central purposes of this architectural complex was the mediation of the living and the dead. Not all processed dead might have ended up in the small charnel house. Some might have been returned, say, to Cahokia for appropriate burial (Milner 1984b). Or perhaps farm families retrieved the bones of their dead. Given the proximity of religious and mortuary buildings at Grossmann and its extraordinary structures—its Ts and sweat lodges in particular—the mediation of the dead, and the healing or ministering to the needs of the living by the special people residing at the site, may have been intimately related.

Other Features

Such intimate relations are evident in the pits, posts, screens, and middens of Grossmann. The first of these are relatively common, at 95 examples, but are outnumbered nonetheless by buildings. Indeed, the house-to-pit ratio at Grossmann, as noted, is unusually high for domestic farmsteads and villages. Pits usually outnumber structures by at least two to one. More-

Figure 4.17. Cross section view of post pit, Grossmann site (extraction and insertion ramps extend to left and right along the two walls, with post mold at the intersection).

over, even given a few large pits, Grossmann's pit storage potential was not great. Nine large pits account for more than half the total pit volume at the site (34 m^3), six of which are associated with the Stirling phase. Moreover, three of the largest pits were located inside two of the T-shaped structures, indicating that the large pits may have had special, nondomestic purposes. Five other large pits contained unusual deposits, discussed in greater detail in the next chapter. A total of 39 pits were less than 20 cm deep; only 15 were 50 cm deep or deeper.

The Grossmann residents did make their pits larger through time. Early Stirling phase pits have the lowest average volume. The middle Stirling phase, by contrast, had both the most and the largest pits (mean = 1 m^3), although this might be a partial function of a longer phase duration. In addition, 6 of the 11 middle Stirling phase pits were inside structures, while none of the 10 late Lohmann phase pits were located inside structures. These trends compare well with the findings of studies that suggest that pits were more likely to be hidden inside structures later in time (Mehrer 1995).

Four freestanding marker posts, similar to those inside the public buildings, measured up to 90 cm in depth (again, note that a 25 cm plow zone was removed, and posts were therefore at least 25 cm deeper than excavated depth indicates). Examination of the profiles suggests that the posts ranged from 40 to 60 cm in diameter, necessitating insertion and extraction ramps. Similar posts are often identified at Cahokia in the centers of courtyards, on or near mounds and plazas, or otherwise marking important locations (Figure 4.17).

As opposed to being prominently marked by upright posts, the loci of greatest activity at Grossmann (discussed in the next chapter) were actually conspicuously shielded by screens. These screens are observed as rows of posts that do not appear to be structure walls. Of 121 posts that were unassociated with structures, there were many isolated posts—perhaps the remains of drying racks or weaving frames—and six linear patterns of four or more posts interpreted to have formed screens. Some of the largest of the screens had 10 or more posts in a line (Figure 4.18). Similar screens have been identified at other Cahokian nodal sites or in Cahokia proper, including atop Monks Mound (Benchley 1974). At Grossmann, all of the screens were situated near event locations. Screens were likely intended to prevent some people from viewing or passing through specific, important areas of the complex during a specific event (see Chapter 5). Such events included the burning of a likely animate flint-clay figurine during a Green Corn ceremony in conjunction with pit F159.

As contrasted with the event-based debris in such pits, 10 features with irregular profiles and uneven bottoms proved to be middens. The middens at Grossmann are here thought to be some sort of semiformal activity areas, which were later filled with trash. They are usually shallow, from 4 to 28 cm deep, and are all located near clusters of houses. One midden, F35, was a deeper depressed area located between and around four pits.

Discussion

The Grossmann site, probably occupied for no more than 50 years, was founded late in the Lohmann phase (ca. A.D. 1075) and was occupied throughout the early Stirling phase. In other words, Grossmann was founded and occupied *after* the Richland Complex farming villages were already emplaced, at about the same time that Cahokia was approaching its early-twelfth-century zenith.

Although Grossmann was located in the midst of thriving Richland Complex farming villages, it looked very little like those farming villages. The suite of T-shaped structures (*N* = 3), council houses (*N* = 4), sweat lodges (*N* = 3), storage buildings (*N* = ca. 24), a mortuary platform, and a charnel house far exceeds anything known from Halliday, Pfeffer,

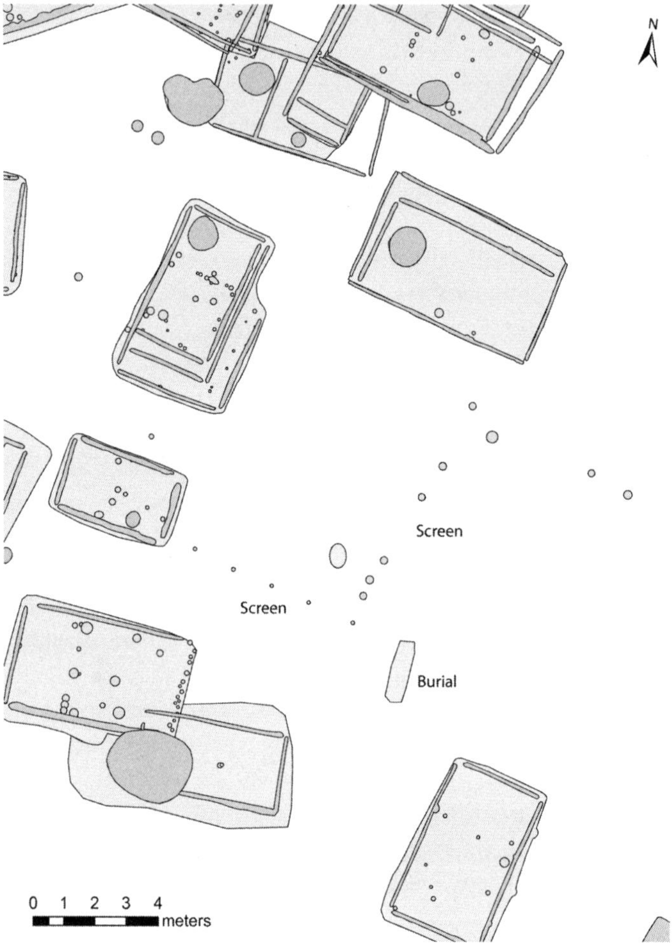

Figure 4.18. Plan view of screen features, Grossmann site.

Knoebel, or Hal Smith. Indeed, Grossmann had more identifiable special-purpose buildings than any other site reported in the region other than Cahokia or East St. Louis proper. Moreover, at least one of each type of building stood at all times in the site's history. As an architectural complex, it may be the ultimate nodal site outside the American Bottom proper.

To be clear, Grossmann was not a "mound center" or a town. Indeed, the nearest such mounded complex, Pfeffer, is strikingly dissimilar to Grossmann in terms of the wide spacing of its pole-and-thatch architecture and the intermittent quality of much of its human occupation (see Chapter 3).

Rather, Grossmann seems more like Cahokia, as if a piece of Tract 15A or East St. Louis were excised and pasted onto the rural Richland landscape. Why would such a piece of Cahokia be emplaced in the midst of the resettled and immigrant farmers of the uplands?

First, several lines of evidence suggest that Grossmann had an unusual proportion of structures devoted solely to storage, and this likely matters greatly in terms of understanding what the people at Grossmann were trying to do (see Figure 4.11). In other words, much of the activity at Grossmann was likely correlated with the need to accumulate upland products so that they could be transferred to Cahokia proper. The architecture of the site might have facilitated such a mission. Certainly, given its location between the two major drainages of the Richland uplands, Grossmann was ideally situated to facilitate the gathering of upland products for transport to Cahokia. The largest population of likely immigrants in the Cahokia region, Halliday's 200 or so people, could have been watched on a daily basis from the hilltop Grossmann site just 1.5 km away. Depending on tree cover, others at Knoebel, Hal Smith, or other unexcavated sites might also have been observable from Grossmann or the crest of a nearby hill. Surplus crops could easily have been packed to Grossmann and, from there, to Cahokia.

Because such produce would have been held only temporarily, storage pits may have been unnecessary beyond the needs of the Grossmann residents. Pits, which provide superior storage over the long term (as they offer temperature and pest control), are less vulnerable to weathering and pilfering. However, for short-term storage, buildings would facilitate both the quick identification of what was stored where and the easy retrieval of the material to be transferred. Thus, storage buildings—for the short-term storage of bulk goods—would have made more sense if Grossmann was a Cahokian nodal or administrative complex.

Second, the large meetinghouses of Grossmann point to another mediating quality of the site. Grossmann's meetinghouses were buildings where farmers could have met to confer with each other and with Cahokians. These buildings have a deep history in the region, and it seems that they were intentionally built in traditional ways, with single-post construction instead of wall trenches. From a distance, their roofs would have been the most visible aspect of the site. The addition of sweat lodges and T structures, which were novel additions to the region in the late eleventh century, would have complemented if not better defined the meaning of the public buildings. Sweat lodges would have provided a place for the necessary preparation, cleansing, and purification for those about to engage in important meetings or sacred events. T-shaped dwellings, as I understand them, would have connected such sacred qualities and events to actual people—the administrators of Grossmann.

Few visitors from any local farming community would have ever seen anything like Grossmann, except upon visiting Cahokia. Here was an extraordinarily compact complex of dozens of pole-and-thatch buildings, upright posts, walls, and human remains. These differences would have immediately provided visual cues that signaled Grossmann's special position vis-à-vis Cahokia and the nearby farming district. Some such cues were exclusionary.

The division of space and the variability in building size, shape, and function do hint that some people, their collective identity, or their actions were marked and then segregated by screens and walls. Perhaps the marking happened primarily through their practices—Grossmann's inhabitants might have included people with distinct ritual-religious responsibilities as well social or political status (this will become more evident in the next chapter when the recovered material culture is discussed). Some elements of the Grossmann architectural setting, such as T-shaped buildings, meetinghouses, and the charnel house, and the occupations and status they represented, would have set certain individuals apart.

Perhaps one might even argue that Grossmann was home to administrators only. Several lines of evidence suggest that despite the large number of buildings at Grossmann, there may not have been very many permanent residents. It was estimated based on construction details that at least one-quarter of the buildings were storage structures, and another set of perhaps 15 structures were public or nondomestic buildings, leaving a maximum of 76 structures (spread out over three 15-year phases) that could have been domiciles. If a stable population is assumed across the three time periods, there could have been no more than 25 actual residences in use at any given point in time (although I suspect fewer were actually domiciles). The low number of pits also suggests a lower permanent population than building numbers suggest, and the possibility exists that only one elite or Cahokian family or extended kin group occupied Grossmann at any one time.

Surely there was a leader or leaders among the residents. Surely there were also knowledgeable specialists needed to properly conduct sweats and other rituals on-site. Possibly there were mortuary specialists to engage the spirits of the dead and to perform the proper rituals for the charnel house. There must have been managers who monitored the trading or tithing as well as the storage of the upland products and whatever materials came from Cahokia. Some people must have maintained the meetinghouses, keeping those areas clean of debris and ready for use. Regardless of whether these roles were embodied by one or many individuals, there were impacts of such an aggregation in farm country, to be explored in the next chapter.

Perhaps the most telling fact in support of my recognition of some sort of historical contingencies among Cahokia, Grossmann, and the Richland Complex is the timing of Grossmann's abandonment. This elaborate overbuilt complex of pole-and-thatch architecture ends, seemingly abruptly, sometime in the middle Stirling phase (ca. A.D. 1150). That ending may correlate with a very important dedicatory pit at Grossmann and also hints that occupants made a final, intentional cleanup of the site, discarding unwanted materials in the basins of a couple of large buildings (see Chapter 5). That this was a time that corresponds with the abandonment of the Richland Complex and the construction of palisade walls at Cahokia and East St. Louis may be telling us that Cahokia could no longer maintain its upland farmers.

5
The Remains of Special Events

Various combinations of the things people used (pots, tools, plants, fabrics, magico-ritual items) and the places they used them (including landscapes, towns, buildings, particular settings) mediate the relationships of complexity and hybridity to history. At a special site such as Grossmann, sets of objects from both mundane activities and specialized ritual practices constitute a unique locus of cultural mediation with larger implications for the formation of a phenomenon such as greater Cahokia. An understanding of that mediation begins with tracing the materials (Weismantel and Meskell 2014). Here I present both general material patterns—focusing on ceramics and lithics—and the specifics of event-based deposits, where the inventories of materials form something more than the sum of their parts. There is a consistency to the diversity of the Grossmann materials that matters with respect to the big picture. Perhaps more than any other line of evidence, the event deposits argue for the role and import of thirdspaces such as Grossmann and its gatherings of people and—even more so—things in the development of Cahokia.

Artifact Assemblages

Rock, mineral, fired clay, and organic materials make up the inventories of most early Mississippian nonfood artifacts in the Cahokia region. At Grossmann, excluding a cache of celts, lithic artifacts account for 34 percent of the recovered materials by weight. This is among the lowest percentages for any site in the region (Figure 5.1). Chert accounts for 38 percent of the lithic material by weight, more than half (52 percent) of

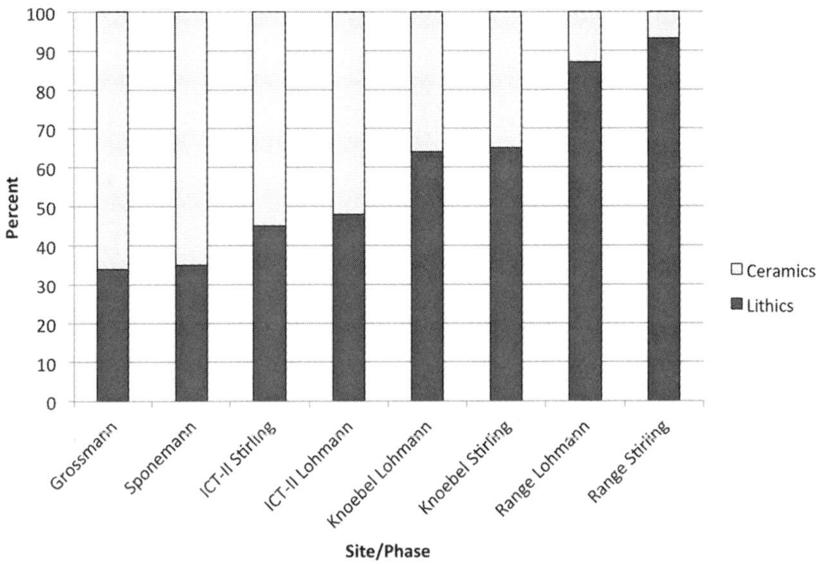

Figure 5.1. Proportion of ceramics versus lithics at Grossmann and other sites. The dark portion of the bars represents lithics, the light color ceramics (data from Alt 2002b; Gums 1993; Hanenberger 2003; Holley 1989; Jackson et al. 1992).

which is Burlington (Tables 5.1 and 5.2). Mill Creek chert, in turn, accounts for 40 percent of that chert, the remainder being a diverse assortment of Cobden, Kaolin, Hixton, Fort Payne, Salem, Ste. Genevieve, and glacial-cobble debitage. Compared to chert, unaltered limestone and sandstone rocks occur at unusually low densities at Grossmann. Most settlements, such as Knoebel, had large amounts of limestone, presumably for the processing of corn, as well as quantities of sandstone and fire-cracked igneous rocks, many ending up lining fireplaces. The lithics, then, parallel the already-reported findings for low-density residential occupation but high-density ritual events.

Although lacking in limestone and sandstone overall, most of the Grossmann lithic material by weight was in fact igneous and metamorphic rock. Among these nonchert lithic artifacts were 317 tools recovered from 77 features. Twenty-two of those features had 5 or more distinct tools each. Seven features contained 10 or more distinct tools. Many of the recovered tools were used for more than one purpose: an igneous cobble might be used as a hammer and a grinder; a piece of sandstone might be used as an abrader as well as a saw and a sander; most sandstone saws also had evidence of use as sanders. If all functional elements of multipurpose tools

Table 5.1. Ground-Stone, Rock, and Mineral Artifact Inventory

Nonchipped stone artifact	Quantity	Weight (g)
Celt	9	3,386.3
Celt cache	70	133,258.8
Celt debitage and flakes	243	2,502.0
Celt fragment hammerstone	1	337.5
Cobble hammerstones/grinders	70	16,818.8
Cobbles and igneous rock	475	8,408.7
Discoidal fragment (Cahokia-style)	1	29.4
Galena	26	167.4
Hematite and ocher	98	1,749.0
Hematite plummet blank (pre-Mississippian)	1	555.6
Igneous cobble palette	1	51.3
Mica	3	1.0
Quartz	55	692.1
Quartz crystal	60	64.2
Sandstone abrader	111	4,393.5
Sandstone discoidal preform	1	64.5
Sandstone palette	12	1,535.5
Sandstone saw	25	365.0
Sedimentary rock*	11,989	141,380.9
Slate pendant (pre-Mississippian)	1	43.0
Total	**13,252**	**315,804.5**

*Count is estimated

are counted, the most common uses for tools at Grossmann were sanding, followed by hammering and abrading.

Concentrations of chert microdrills ($N = 13$) and celt-making debitage point to restricted crafting activities being the source of the site's more general tool assemblage. For instance, microdrills were concentrated in one structure (F234), with a second set of microdrills located in the isolated eastern workshop feature cluster. Presumably these were used in the drilling of materials, including marine shell, for the production of beads or bead necklaces (Pauketat 1993). Twenty-eight features contained some sort of celt-making or celt-sharpening debris. Nine of those features had more than three such artifacts. An adjacent Lohmann phase building at the Stohlmann site, 100 m east of Grossmann, had even more (Jackson 2000). Celt production, using raw basalt and diabase from the St. Francois Mountains, has been identified at only a few sites in the Cahokia region, and within those sites evidence is concentrated (Pauketat and Alt 2004). In the case of the sub-Mound 51 pit at Cahokia, its presence suggests that

Table 5.2. Chipped Stone Artifact Inventory

Chipped stone artifact	Quantity	Weight (g)
Burlington drills and microdrills	37	34.1
Cahokia, Hayes, Bayougoula points	19	36.9
Chert flake tools and debitage	12,359	26,721.6
Chert hammers/grinders	5	966.1
Mill Creek/Burlington adze fragments	6	333.3
Mill Creek hoe blades/fragments	13	4,012.6
Mill Creek hoe flakes	9,214	11,385.1
Miscellaneous projectile point fragments	24	164.1
Ramey knife fragments	4	32.4
Total	**21,681**	**43,686.2**

celt production took place during ritual events. The same seems possible for the limited production of celts or the burial of celt preforms at Pfeffer and Knoebel (see Chapter 3).

Given that celts and celt-making debitage occurred in 9 percent of the site features (most notably in a celt cache), it is reasonable to consider the possibility that many of the site's lithic tools relate in some way to celt production. Hammers, grinders, and sanders are all reasonable suspects for celt production. If these tools were used in specific tool sets for celt production, it would appear that the various elements were not discarded as a unit. It does, however, suggest that if a set of tools was used to create objects for rituals, it was not necessary to discard those tools afterward. This may also suggest that given the multiple tasks for which most Mississippian tools were used, there is no reason to expect a discrete tool set. Rather, the tool assemblage seems to derive from the seamless mix of ordinary and extraordinary happenings at the site.

Fired Clay and Pottery

The same might be said of pots, pottery trowels, spindle whorls, and a ceramic earspool. A total of 769 distinct ceramic vessels could be distinguished at Grossmann, which happens to be more vessels, of more kinds, than have been found at most other known upland sites (Figure 5.2). For example, Grossmann's pots included more beakers, effigy bottles, and Ramey Incised jars than any of the previously mentioned Richland sites (see Chapter 3).

A few of the ceramic vessels at Grossmann were unidentifiable as to type or origin because of unusual construction and decorative treatments

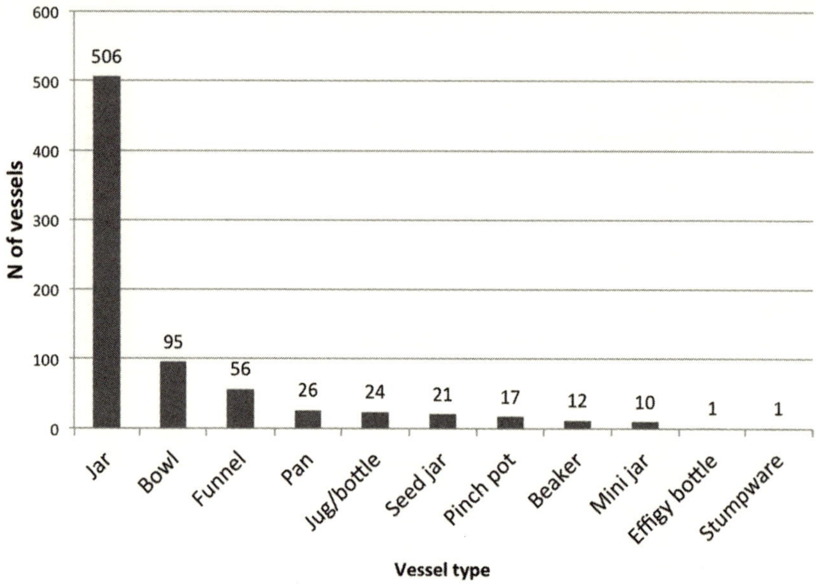

Figure 5.2. Bar chart showing relative frequency of pottery vessel types, Grossmann site.

possibly connected to their ritual purposes. Among these were a vulture effigy bowl (from F198), portions of bottles shaped like human bodies (from F198 and F234), and jars with scalloped, S-shaped lips, punctates, and incised designs (Figure 5.3). Some features on these vessels are reminiscent of known types, such as the S-shaped lips (O'Brien 1969), but the overall rim designs did not fit any known type and were not recognized by analysts working in nearby regions. Such vessels are apparent hybrids or experimental designs, not copied by later potters, though possibly desirable for certain events.

Most of the vessels were jars, of which 96, 3, and 1 percent were shell, grog, and limestone tempered, respectively. Slips were applied to more than half of the Grossmann jars, fewer than at Cahokia (64 vs. 88 percent) during the Lohmann and Stirling phases (Pauketat 1998a), but more than at Halliday (ca. 40 percent) or Knoebel (52 percent of Stirling phase jars) (Alt 2002b). That is, Grossmann ceramic-slip trends fall somewhere between those of Cahokia and those of the upland sites, most closely resembling the nodal BBB Motor site. Likewise, the Grossmann jar rim shapes, as revealed in their "lip-protrusion" indices, are closer to Cahokian forms than they are to other upland jars (Figure 5.4). That is, the Grossmann pots are more Cahokian in character, regardless of where they were made.

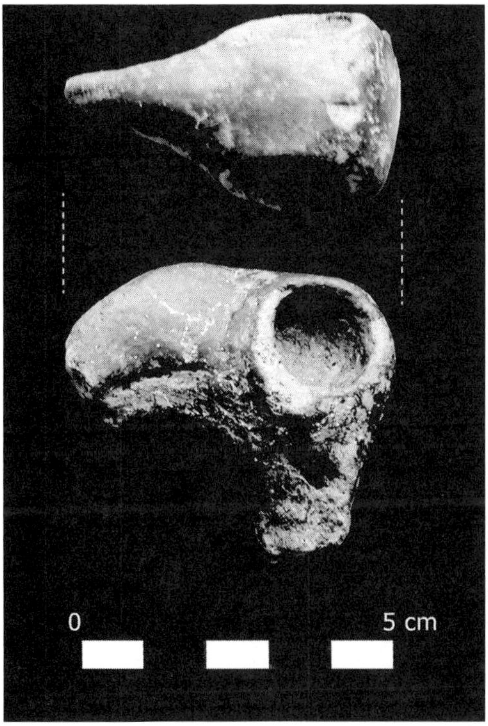

Figure 5.3. Vulture effigy head adorno from pottery bowl.

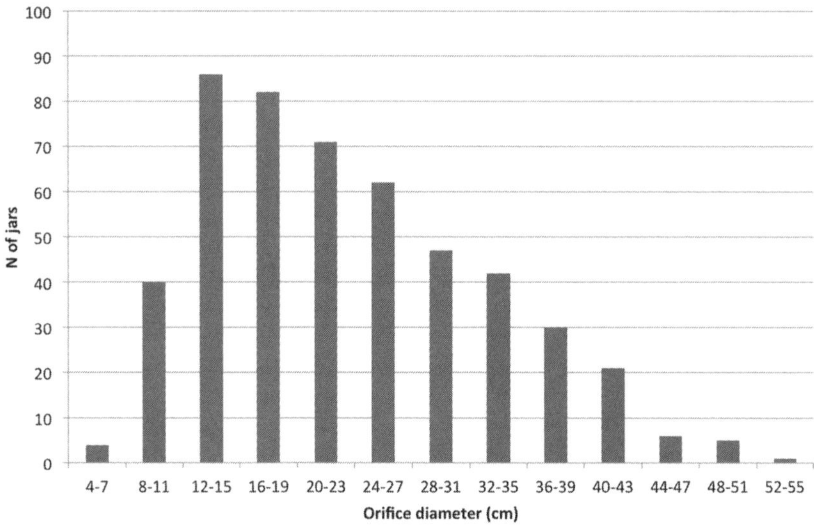

Figure 5.4. Bar chart showing jar sizes at Grossmann.

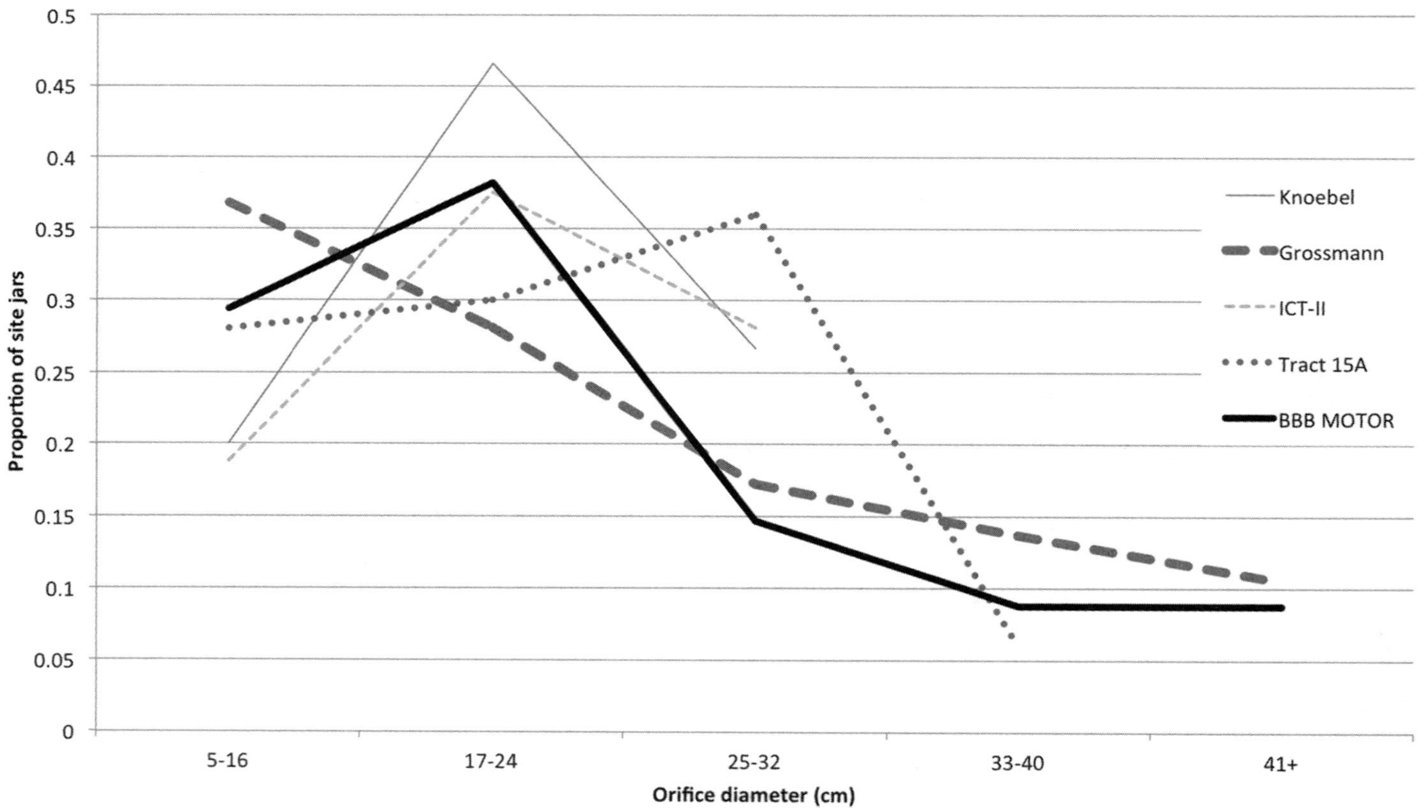

Figure 5.5. Jar size distributions from select sites (data from Alt 2002b; Emerson and Jackson 1984; Holley 1989; Pauketat 1998a).

The size distribution of Grossmann jars is equally distinct. American Bottom assemblages typically exhibit clear peaks—two to four modes—indicating greater quantities of midsized cooking jars. The Grossmann jar size modes, however, were positively skewed toward small sizes, a pattern that would be even more extreme if the 17 pinch pots were added to the small jar category (Figure 5.5). Similarly, as only 25 percent of the recovered jars had any evidence of cooking soot on them, and no more than 62 percent were within the size range of typical cooking jars (≥ 14 cm and ≤ 35 cm), it seems likely that some subset of jars—at least 25 to 38 percent—were not used for everyday domestic purposes. Thus, the Grossmann resident population may have been much lower than the dense stand of architectural constructions suggests.

Again, the largest jars were probably used for storage, while the smallest may have been used for drinks, potions, special relishes or sauces, and individual servings (Figure 5.6). Emerson (1989) has previously suggested that the Black Drink, made from the exotic yaupon holly plant (*Ilex vomitoria*), may have been dispensed for consumption in both small jars and Ramey Incised jars, in conjunction with beakers. Representing just 6 percent of the jars, the proportion of Ramey ceramics at Grossmann was lower than at Cahokia or other ceremonial nodes on the floodplain (Emerson and Jackson 1984; Holley 1989; Jackson et al. 1992; Pauketat 1998a, 2013a). Grossmann's Ramey Incised jars were also smaller than average. The average orifice diameter for the Ramey jars at Grossmann was 19 cm, while the average diameter for all jars was 23 cm. By comparison, Tract 15A's Ramey jars averaged 23 cm in diameter, almost as large as an average-sized cooking jar. This fits a pattern identified by Pauketat and Emerson (1991), who determined that the occurrence and size of Ramey pottery decreased with distance from Cahokia. But then again, the Grossmann vessel assemblage is skewed toward specialty vessels, possibly affecting the size distribution at Grossmann. Perhaps confirming this possibility, the distribution of Ramey Incised ceramics within the Grossmann site points to a concentration at the site's center. Five of the 18 Ramey Incised vessels were located in the same house basin, F198, an oversized structure in the center of the site. The remaining Ramey sherds were just north and south of F198.

That these were used in the dispensation of the Black Drink is uncertain (Emerson 1989). However, recent chemical tests have verified the presence of the biomarkers of yaupon holly in 1 of the 12 Grossmann beakers (this was the only one tested from Grossmann) (Crown et al. 2012). These were variously tempered with shell and fine grog, slipped ($N = 6$), and decorated (3 at Grossmann with incising). Their elaborate and often

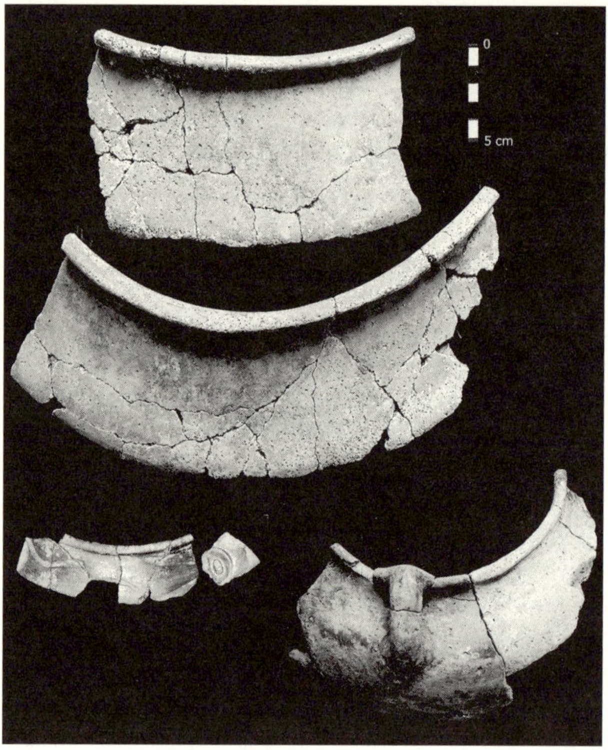

Figure 5.6. Select jars from Grossmann: top, two large rims from F146; bottom left, Ramey Incised jar from F179; bottom right, jar with loop handles from F275.

finely made appearance indicates their use in religious ceremony. At Grossmann, these beakers were found in deposits also containing galena, quartz crystals, hematite, and, in one case, human leg bones. Others were included in event deposits (discussed later in this chapter).

Seed jars and funnels might have been used in performances as well. The former, a minority vessel form at Grossmann, presumably served in a storage capacity, based both on their absence of use wear and sooting and on their higher frequency at Cahokia. Funnels would seem unlikely to have been used in ritual spectacle and were probably used in the production of lye for processing maize into hominy (Benchley 2003). However, 8 percent of the vessels at Grossmann were funnels, a figure higher than that of most areas of Cahokia, Cahokia's outliers, and upland farming villages (Emerson and Jackson 1984; Holley 1989; Pauketat 1998a). Only the

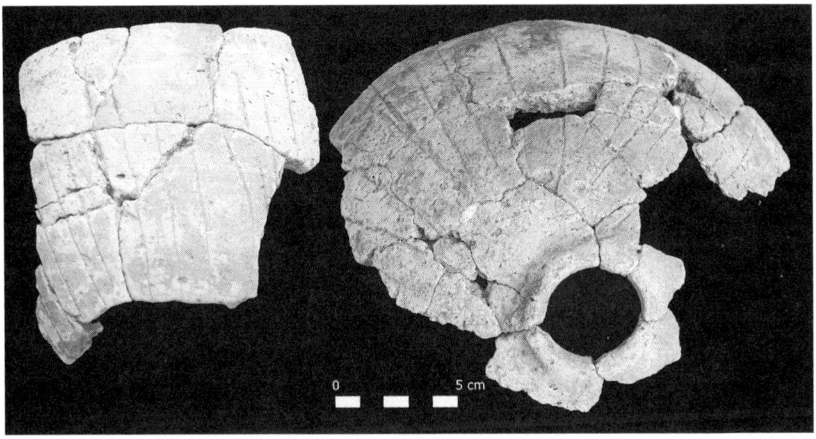

Figure 5.7. Upper and lower sections of two ceramic funnels (F146 and F229).

Mississippian component settlement at the Range site had a similar concentration of funnels (Hanenberger 2003).

Moreover, funnels at the site were recovered from extraordinary event deposits in concentrations: 56 funnels from 30 features. Perhaps this bespeaks the association of hominy with Grossmann's events. But it may also be that funnels were, in this case, used as strainers for the Black Drink, which was made by steeping holly leaves and stems in hot water and then straining the tea out of the steeping pot, perhaps using something like the strainer described by Hudson (1976:228): "To make black drink the Indians first dried the leaves and twigs and put them in an earthen container and parched them over a fire to a dark brown color. This roasting made the caffeine more soluble; coffee beans are roasted for the same reason. They placed the roasted twigs and leaves in water and boiled it until it was a dark brown liquid. The drink was then poured through a strainer and into vessels to cool."

A funnel, which is basically a conical or bulb-shaped ceramic tube with a constricted opening at both ends, could have been fitted with a fabric, leather, or wooden screen and would have served very well as a strainer (Figure 5.7). It is also possible that a fabric bag, such as those identified burned in ritual deposits at Grossmann, was placed in the funnel and the brew poured in such that the liquid would pass through the fabric covering the open bottom and into a beaker, with the netting catching the leaves and stems.

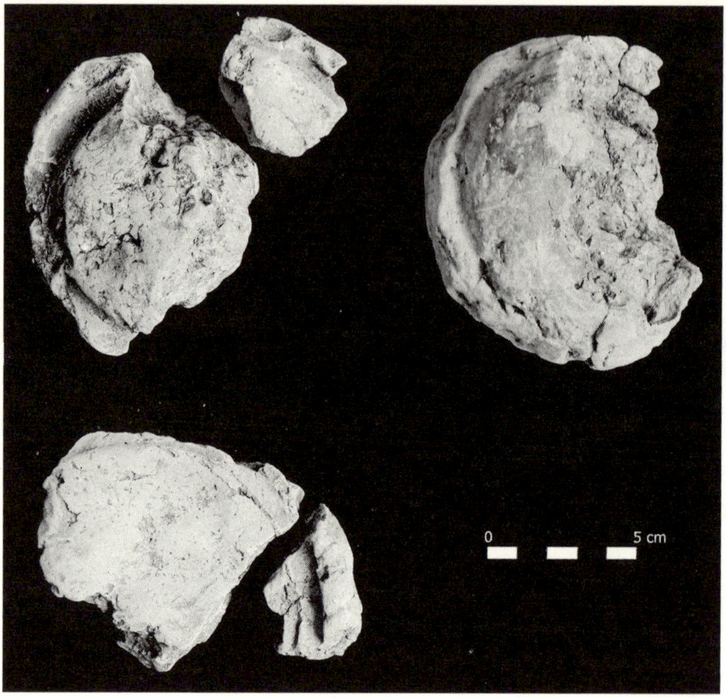

Figure 5.8. Plan view of fired clay plugs from F281 (lower left), F234 (upper left), and F256 (upper right).

Special Objects and Producers?

Among such events attested by pottery remains may have been the annual opening of sealed containers of pourable seeds or special potions. Nine whole or partial fired-clay vessel plugs, most from one late Lohmann phase pit, were recognized among the burned debris from Grossmann, indicating that these had been tossed into fires and hardened (Figure 5.8). These are nearly identical to objects from southeastern Missouri known as Kersey Clay Objects (Marshall 1965; Million 1980; O'Brien 2001). The imprints on the Grossmann clay objects, oval impressions 10–12 cm in diameter, match the orifice diameters of the larger mode of ceramic jugs (Figures 5.9 and 5.10). The 19 jugs and 5 other bottles at Grossmann were storage vessels, perhaps similar in use to seed jars, and seeds have previously been suggested as the material stored inside.

Aside from the clay bottle stoppers, there are two other kinds of clay items that also warrant mention. The first is another type of ceramic

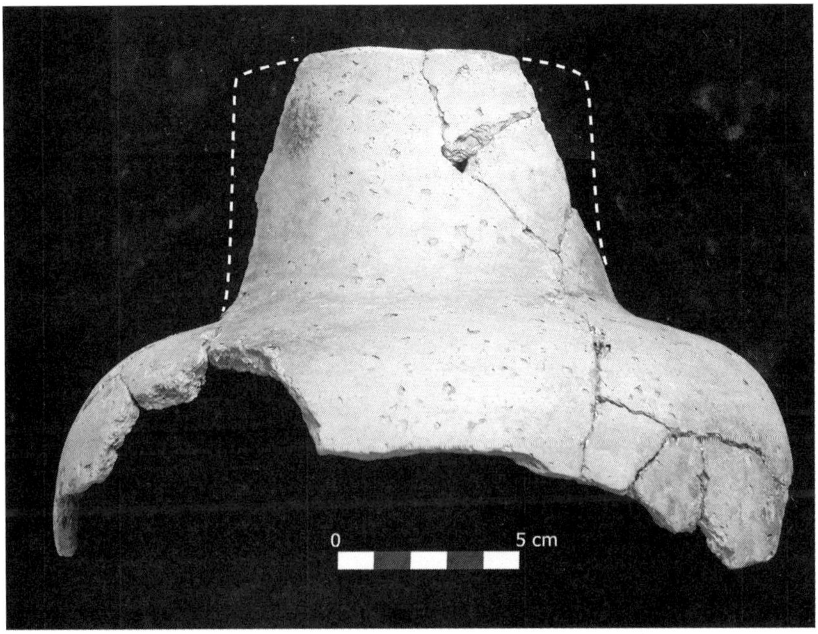

Figure 5.9. Side view of pottery jug from F209.

utility item simply called fired-clay objects (FCOs). The second is fabric-impressed burned clay.

As described by Douglas Jackson (2004), FCOs are irregular rounded forms with smoothed surfaces. Jackson examined 417 such objects and suggested that they were used in place of rocks as heating elements. There are 367 pieces of FCOs at Grossmann, many associated with a single hearth (Figure 5.11). Not surprisingly, there is a high correlation between deposits of FCOs at Grossmann and deposits of burned materials, but a spatial analysis is more revealing. That is, the southern edge of the site contained twice as many FCOs (by weight) as the rest of the site, although that area accounts for less than a quarter of Grossmann's features, and even less than 25 percent of the recovered material. However, all three of the sweat lodges are located in this southern area, and the concentration of fired-clay objects is likely related to their use in the sweat lodge hearths.

Other fired pieces of clay retain the impressions of fabric. Pit feature 287 contained small bits of the burned remains of fabrics, but it also contained impressions of these fabrics on soils that were pressed into the pit on top of and under the burning fabric. The heat of the covered burning materials fired these pieces and preserved the imprints of the fabric. All

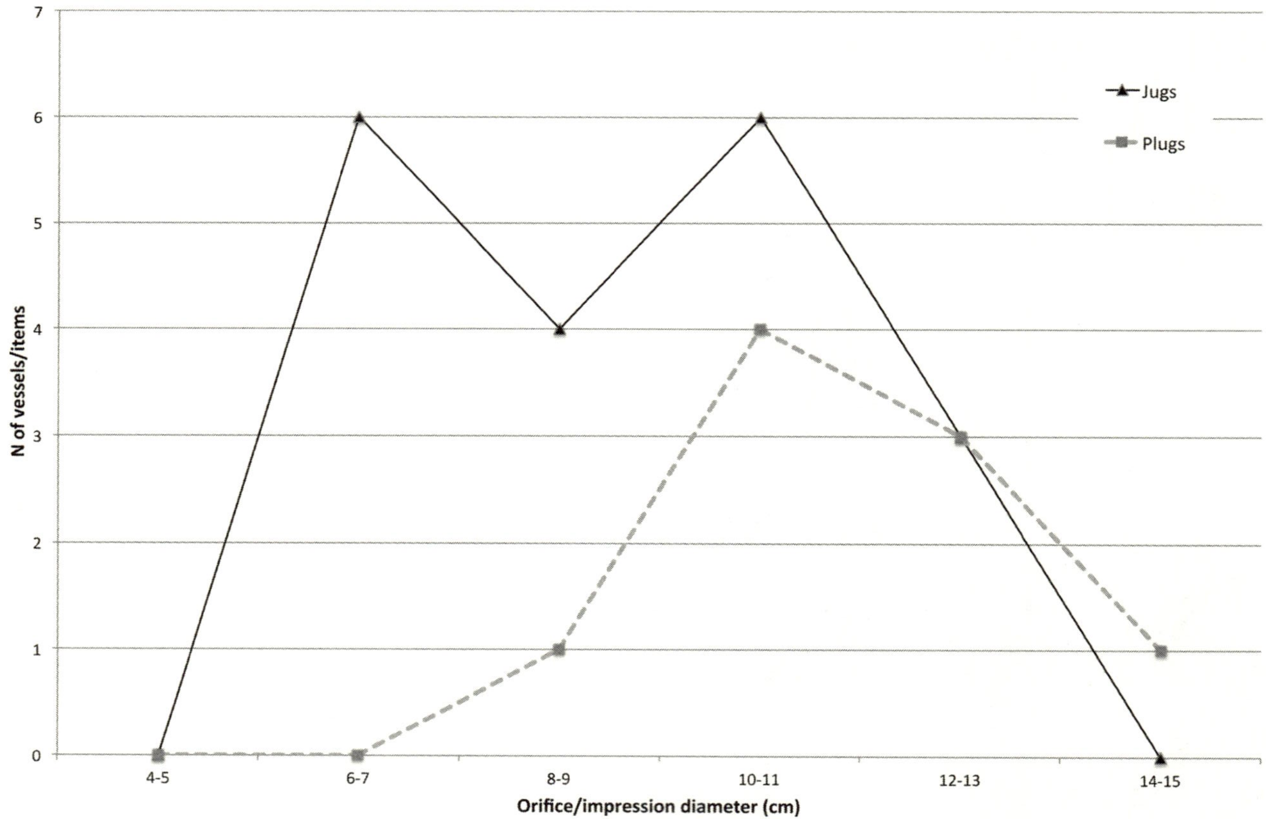

Figure 5.10. Graph showing orifice diameters of clay plugs versus pottery jugs.

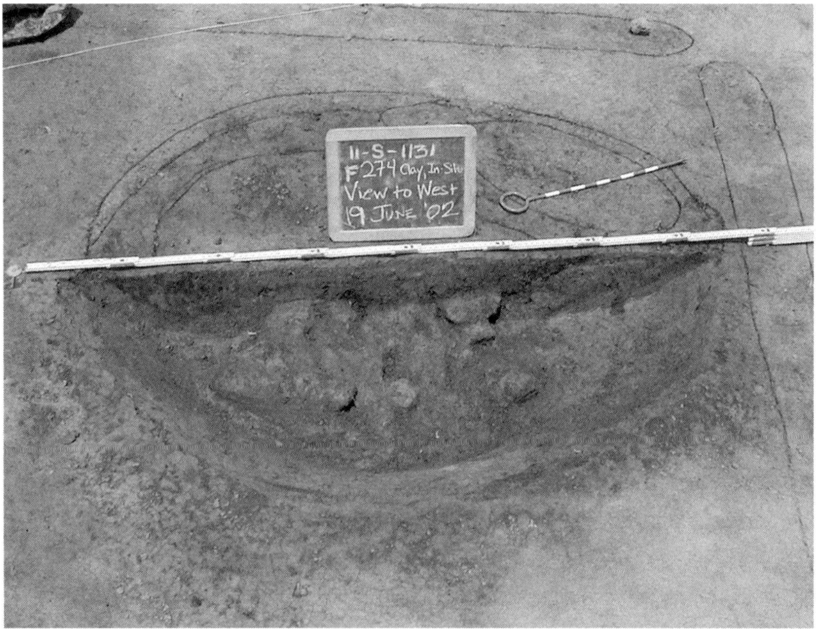

Figure 5.11. Fired-clay objects in situ, Grossmann site.

of the imprinted clay pieces but one were located in F287. The one other fragment of fabric-impressed clay was located in pit F298, inside a structure on the northern edge of the site. All are indicative of special events.

One small (2.2 cm diameter) ceramic earspool was recovered from a midden (F236) near houses F234 and F240 (Figure 5.12). The earspool was made from clay mixed with a very fine shell temper, and coated with a red slip exterior. The size and shape are similar to those of a flint-clay earspool recovered from the Olszewski site (Jackson and Hanenberger 1990). Earspools are very rarely recovered archaeologically. High-status individuals presumably wore them in pairs. In later Mississippian imagery, earspools are shown being worn by leaders, warriors, and religious specialists (Phillips and Brown 1978). Nearly all earspools that have been recovered archaeologically from the Cahokia region came from ridge-top mound-burial associations at and around Cahokia proper (Ahler and DePuydt 1987; Baires 2014; Fowler et al. 1999).

High-status people or specialists could have managed or been involved in the production of the materials, clothing, and things used in Grossmann rituals. For instance, 34 whole or partial spindle whorls were recovered

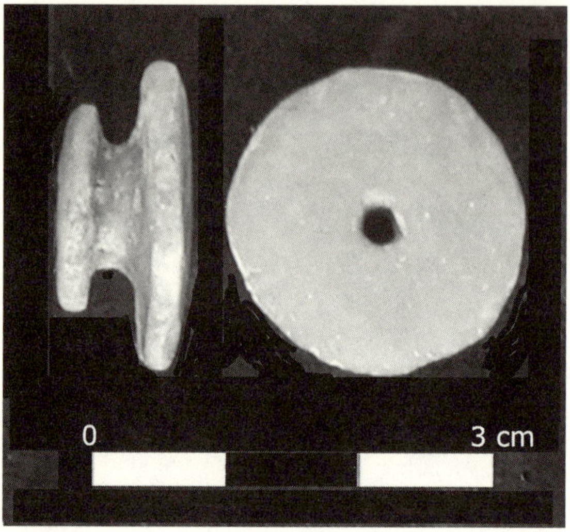

Figure 5.12. Pottery earspool (F236), Grossmann site.

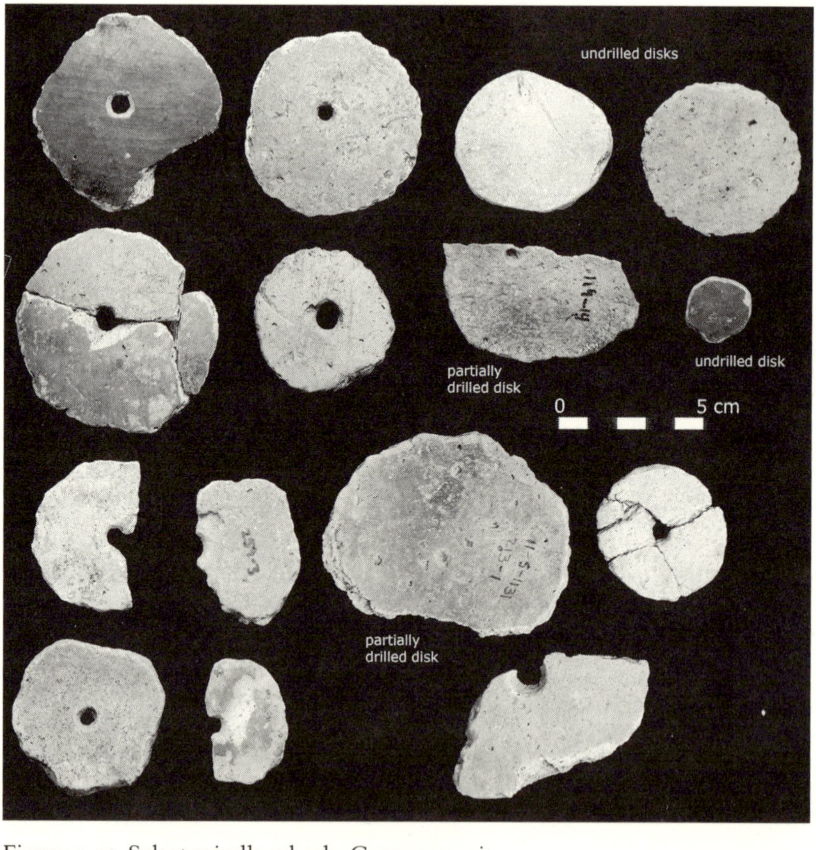

Figure 5.13. Select spindle whorls, Grossmann site.

from Grossmann. So too were many charred bits of cordage and sections of fabric, owing in part to the many burned lenses within Grossmann features. In an earlier study, I found that spindle whorls were concentrated in certain settlements, and within those settlements, they had a tendency to be concentrated in only a few deposits (Alt 1999). The highest density of such whorls in the region is found at the Halliday and Knoebel sites, near Grossmann (see Chapter 3), but Grossmann's 34 items may yet constitute a high density given the few people suspected to have lived at the site. However, the 34 items could be another by-product of the ritual events, possibly indicating the presence of Richland spinners on-site (Figure 5.13).

Likewise, two pottery trowels—fired ceramic tools used for shaping the walls of ceramic vessels—were found at Grossmann. In this case, it is not the density but the context that is informative. One partial pottery trowel was recovered from pit F256, a feature with special-event deposits (see the following subsection). A second was recovered (during the stripping of features in the western cluster by ITARP) in an area that also produced other craft materials (celt flakes, abraders, and grinders). As pottery trowels are not common at Cahokian sites, it may be that they are not everyday household tools but are more likely to have been used by specialists.

Event Deposits

Beyond evidence of crafting events, the Grossmann site also had a higher density of suggestive exotic materials, including projectile points, quartz crystals, pigment stones, and Mill Creek chert, that hint at event-related deposition. Of these, quartz crystals and pigment stones were highly desirable magico-ritual items originating from as far afield as the Ouachita Mountains in northern Arkansas or as near as the uplands beyond the northern American Bottom (Kelly 1980). These were often concentrated, as in 52 shattered pieces of geode, cracked open to remove the quartz crystals inside, which were recovered from five features clustered in two discrete locations around F179 and F235 at Grossmann. The same applies to Mill Creek chert, a ubiquitous exotic and the raw material for hoe, adze, and knife blades made in far southern Illinois (Cobb 1989, 2000). Although hoe resharpening flakes were recovered from numerous features across the Grossmann site, a large amount of burned Mill Creek chert was recovered from burning events in special-event deposits, indicating that several entire hoes had been incorporated into these ceremonies. Three more complete and intact hoes were also recovered from pits F161 and F84 (within T structure F6).

Whether hoe-blade offerings burned in a fire or craft debris left on a surface, many of the Grossmann materials appear to derive from discrete ceremonial events. A key feature of these events was the burning of different kinds of objects and materials—magico-religious items, foods, and tools—frequently in conjunction with roof thatch. These were intentional incinerations as signaled by the extreme heat of fires involved in the immolation of the objects. The heat was intense enough in some cases to deeply discolor the soils around the deposits, to shatter stone, and to warp sections of pottery vessels.

The events had in common a suite of objects such as exotic minerals, quartz crystals, nondomestic pottery, killed tools (hoes and knives), craft production tools (hammers, abraders, saws), curated objects (pre-Mississippian points), burned thatch, and burned fabric (associated with corn or seeds). Other unusual deposits contained large amounts of burned materials but lacked diagnostic items (Table 5.3). Also lacking were the diagnostic components of feasting as seen at Cahokia (Pauketat et al. 2002). There were no serving platters or bowls and no concentrations of meat-bearing animal bones.

Late Lohmann Phase

An open courtyard between Lohmann phase structures F234, F235, F240, and F266 was the scene of several repeated special events that left behind traces in both pits and structure basins (Figure 5.14). The four building basins and three pits in the center of this area contained nearly a quarter of all pottery found at the site. The greatest concentrations of trash in the house basins and pits were in the section of the feature that was closest to the courtyard, confirming that the deposits originated in the courtyard. In its center were three pits (F256, F260, and F275) filled with event-related deposits: burned pots, tools, and the flint-clay figurine pipe, all intermixed with burned fabric, burned corn, and charred seeds.

The heat-exploded flint-clay pipe was located in 2,583 bits and pieces (weighing 2,362.7g) scattered throughout the burned matrix of all major fill zones in pit F275. Up to half of the figurine pipe is missing, but the few reattached pieces suggest a owl's beak and eyes, a winged back with some indication of feathers and the pipe bowl, and a base showing talons (Figure 5.15). The pipe bits and large amounts of burned corn and seeds adhering to the remnants of burned fabric in the pit were deposited among burned wood and thatch in a 20 cm thick layer of fill that was more ash and charcoal than earth (Figure 5.16). Burned mud dauber nests (380.3 g) were presumably originally attached to the thatch of a building. An abrader, an igneous stone grinder, 12 sandstone sanders, 2 sandstone palettes/sanders, 5 heat-distorted jar sections, 4 saws/sanders, and 1 projectile point of an

Table 5.3. Event Deposits in Pits

Feature No.	Size (m)	Depth (m)	Volume (m^3)	Ceramics	Tools (lithic and ceramic)	Other
F12	1.07 × 1.06	0.44	0.28	11 vessels 8 jars avg. diameter 21.25 cm 1 seed jar 1 bowl 1 beaker	1 abrader 1 hoe fragment	human leg bones
F 146	1.62 × 1.58	0.53	1.07	30 vessels 16 jars avg. diameter 25.7 cm 5 funnels 1 jug 1 beaker 6 bowls (1 bowl is incised)	8 saws/sanders 1 Archaic biface 2 hoe fragments	burned thatch burned nuts, seeds, corn mud dauber nests 41 kaolin flakes 3 chunks galena 6 celt flakes
F 159	1.3 × 1.3	1.02	1.42	22 vessels 12 jars avg. diameter 22.17 cm frog effigy handle 2 bowls 7 funnels 1 pan	2 abraders 3 hammerstones	burned thatch, mud dauber nests killed (heat-deformed) pots hoe shatter 2 pieces galena 1 quartz crystal
F 206	0.84 × 0.84	0.19	0.1019		70 complete celts	

Continued on the next page

Table 5.3 *Continued*

Feature No.	Size (m)	Depth (m)	Volume (m^3)	Ceramics	Tools (lithic and ceramic)	Other
F 209	1.6 × 1.51	0.98	1.86	15 vessels 7 jars avg. diameter 20.71 cm 3 bowls (1 bowl is bilobed) 1 seed jar 1 jug 1 funnel 1 bottle 1 pan	4 hammer/grindstones 3 abraders 1 grindstone 1 Madison point	in situ burning 7 quartz crystals burned thatch burned mud dauber nests hematite chunks
F 220	1.63 × 1.62	1.2	2.47	9 vessels 8 jars avg. diameter 23.62 cm 1 bowl	2 hammers 3 palettes	human burial with celt fragment, 1 galena 1 limonite 1 red ocher 1 flake Hixton silicified
F 256	2.42 × 1.35	0.95	2.65	47 vessels 35 jars avg. diameter 22.51 cm 1 mini jar 2 pinch pots 2 seed jars 1 beaker 3 bowls 3 funnels 3 spindle whorls 1 pottery trowel 6 bottle stoppers	1 abrader 1 grindstone 1 hammer 1 sander 2 Cahokia points 2 Ramey knife segments	yellow clay plaster lined 1 hematite 1 red ocher 4 crystals 2 kaolin flakes 6 basalt celt flakes heat-exploded jar

F 260	1.37 × 1.02	0.54	0.82	3 jars avg. diameter 23.3 cm 1 incised sherd	1 hammer burned hoe	1 heat-exploded stone figurine fragment 1 large quartz crystal burned bags of corn and seeds burned thatch mud dauber nests
F 275	2.32 × 1.58	0.62	1.78	5 vessels 4 jars avg. diameter 24.5 cm (1 jar is white slipped) 1 bowl	1 abrader 1 grindstone 12 sanders 2 palettes/sanders 1 projectile point 4 saws/sanders	2,583 fragments heat-killed figurine heat-distorted jar burned fabric burned seeds and corn mud dauber nests
F 287	1.22 × 1.01	0.82	0.78	15 vessels 11 jars avg. diameter 20.73 cm 3 bowls 1 beaker 1 spindle whorl	1 celt butt 1 abrader/sander 2 hammer/ grindstones	burned corn, nuts, and seeds burned fabric bag/basket burned bone 1 quartz crystal fabric-impressed clay chunks

Figure 5.14. Plan map showing event deposits from the Lohmann phase, Grossmann site.

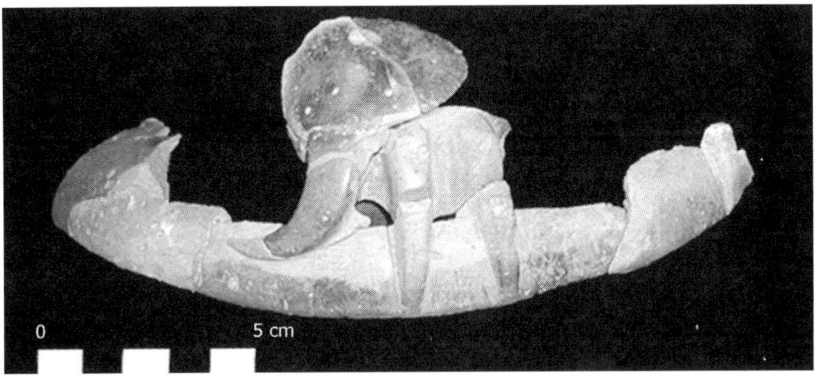

Figure 5.15. Fragment of owl effigy flint-clay smoking pipe, Grossmann site.

Figure 5.16. Profile of event pit F275.

unknown type were also found in this pit. One of the 4 jars (average diameter 24.5 cm) had a white slip. The single recovered bowl fragment was incised. After the pit was partially infilled with the above-described material, it was filled with soil containing more typical domestic debris and then was capped with nearly sterile soil.

Feature 260, a pit less than 3 m south of the just-described F275, also contained a fragment from the carved stone figurine pipe and thus was likely infilled as part of the same or a closely related event. The F260 pit

Figure 5.17. Profile of event pit F260.

was smaller than F275 and produced less material overall, including fewer ceramics. The pit did follow the same depositional pattern, however, with an intensely burned zone of material capped with a layer of sterile fill (Figure 5.17). As in F275, the lowest zone consisted of ash and charcoal. Material recovered in this pit included the rims of three jars and a piece of a unique incised pot. The pieces of the largest vessel had been used to line the pit. There was also a large (8.2 g) quartz crystal and pieces of a burned Mill Creek–chert hoe blade (1,434.5 g). An isolated post less than 1 m north of F260 may have marked the pit's location.

The third pit, F256, was located 7 m west of the other two. This pit was rectangular in plan, like F260 and F275, but much larger (2.45 × 1.35 cm). It was similarly capped with sterile soil but was further distinguished by having a specially prepared yellow clay lining on its floor, similar to special buildings in the uplands, possibly segregating sacred and profane realms (see Chapter 3). In its fill were an abrader, a grindstone, a hammer, a sander,

3 spindle whorls and a pottery trowel, and the sherds of 47 vessels (35 jars, 3 bowls, 2 pinch pots, 2 seed jars, 1 beaker, 3 funnels, and 6 bottle stoppers). One jar appeared killed, indicating its association with a courtyard ceremonial event. There were also the remains of 2 bifacial (i.e., Ramey) knife segments, 2 Cahokia points, traces of pigment, 4 quartz crystals, 2 Kaolin chert flakes, and 6 basalt flakes derived from knapping a celt.

The structures arrayed around these three pits contained additional large amounts of lithic debris and diagnostic pottery, one vessel rim from F234 refitted to a vessel in F256. There was a cache of 13 microdrills, 5 projectile points, 1 sandstone chunkey stone, 9 hammerstones, 1 grinder, 5 sanders, 3 spindle whorls, and a few flakes of celt-making debitage. There was also a screaming-head water-bottle hood fragment, a vulture effigy adorno broken off a bowl, quartz crystals, galena, hematite pigment (416 g), and the distal end of a radius from an extinct *Bison antiquus*. A deposit of cobbles, small rocks, and pebbles covered a patch of the F234 building floor closest to the area of the event pits. Nearby, building F235 contained large amounts of the exotic Kaolin chert (76 flakes) as well as bits of Hixton silicified sediment, pieces of pigment, quartz crystals, 5 chert projectile points, 2 Ramey knife segments, 2 sanders, 2 grinders, 1 spindle whorl, and 1 Archaic-period slate pendant. The ceramic assemblage for this feature included 16 jars, 4 pinch pots, 4 bowls, 1 pan, 1 jug, 1 funnel, and 1 seed jar.

Two or perhaps three screens were set up in and around the features in the Lohmann phase courtyard. One was placed between pits F260 and F275, while the second, more elaborate screen would have separated the rest of the village from the courtyard. The placement of houses and screens would have segregated this area of special events from the view of every other household in the village. A third, shorter row of posts may have been the remains of another screen just north of F256 or, more likely, the location of a small, frequently reset marker post. Just inside the western screen was a robust extended human burial of indeterminate age and sex, cranium located toward the southwest end of the grave (Eve Hargrave, personal communication 2002). To the south of that individual was the charnel house, where the comingled skeletal portions of 18 other men, women, and children were found (see Chapter 4).

Early Stirling Phase

Superimposing pit F159 was pit F161. In it was a complete Mill Creek hoe blade (Figure 5.18). This had been laid in offering on the floor just at the point where the pit cut through the dark fills of the earlier pit F159

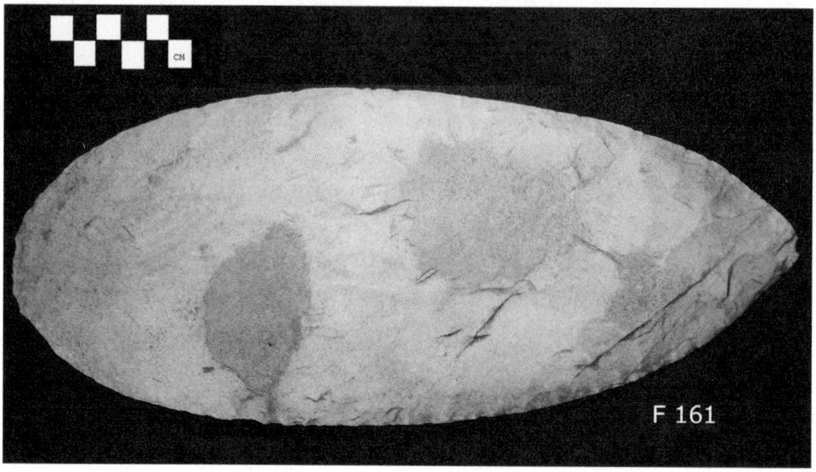

Figure 5.18. Mill Creek–chert hoe blade.

(Figure 5.19). Both occupied the center of another courtyard-like configuration dating to the Stirling phase (Figure 5.20). And both, like the earlier Lohmann phase event-based pits, contained the burned remains of ritual events. Indeed, the heavily oxidized walls of F161 indicated that the burning took place in the pit itself. Incorporated into its fill were the sherds of a jar with a frog effigy handle, 11 other jars, 2 bowls, 7 funnels, and 1 pan. There were also 4 hammers/grinders, 3 abraders, 1 grinder, chert debitage, 1 chipped-chert projectile point, hematite, galena, quartz crystals, and impressive amounts of burned chert, burned thatch, and mud dauber nests (1,263.1 g). Out of the pit's total of 1.8 kg of chert, 1.7 kg consisted of pieces of a burned and exploded Mill Creek–chert hoe blade.

West of F159 was a marker post, and beyond that a screen 8 m long. Similar to the larger of the Lohmann event screens, this screen had a roughly north-south orientation. North of the screen was a larger marker post, and beyond that a dense stand of structures. The deposits in pit F139, west of pit F159, may be related to the same event that created the deposits in pit F159. In it were 4 projectile points, 3 palettes, 1 abrader, flakes of exotic cherts, 1 small crystal, and fragments of 4 ceramic jars and 2 large pans. A house basin at the south end of this courtyard, F178, contained a dumping episode in the northeast corner that consisted of burned materials and other debris that was unlike the material in the rest of the basin and matched the ceremonial debris in pits F139 and F159. Here was more

Figure 5.19. Mill Creek–chert hoe blade in situ on floor of F161.

burned material: galena, exotic chert, pigment stones, a hoe blade fragment, sanders and abraders, and jar fragments (a white-clay pot, a Ramey Incised jar, a fine-incised jar, a jar with a frog effigy handle, and several very small jars).

To the west of house basin F178 was a meetinghouse, and to the east stood a T-shaped structure superimposed by two large pits. The southern-

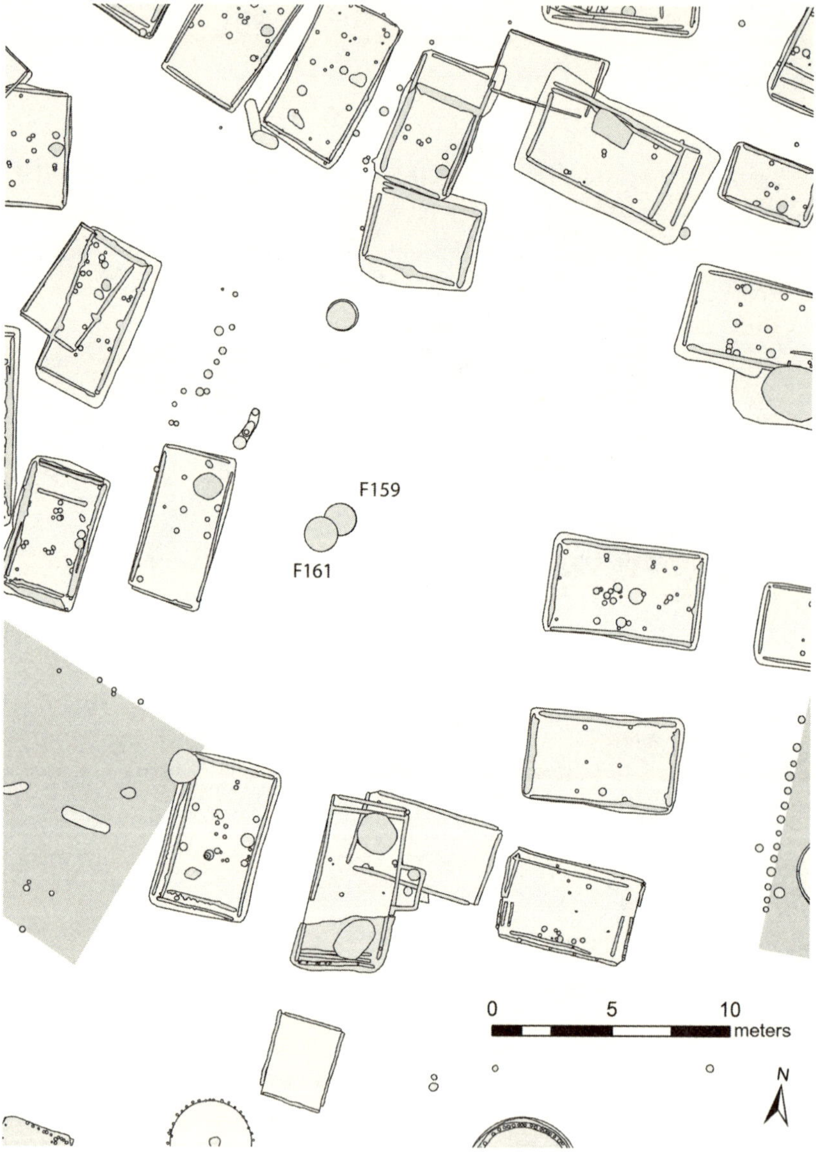

Figure 5.20. Plan map showing event deposits from the Stirling phase, Grossmann site.

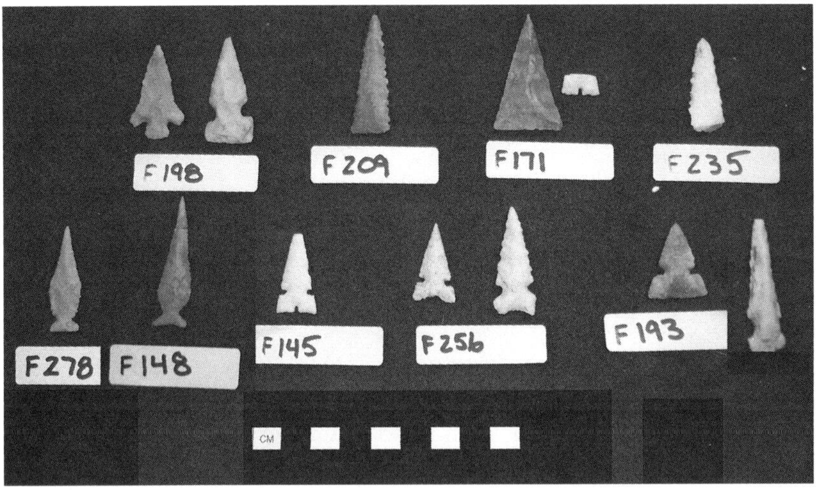

Figure 5.21. Select chipped stone projectile points, Grossmann site.

most pit contained two complete hoe blades and other stone tools. The more northern pit contained the flexed remains of the adult female noted in Chapter 4.

Other Stirling Phase

Five other features warrant mention, including F12, a small pit containing right and left human femurs, and F198, a large house basin that contained most of the site's Ramey Incised vessels. F12 was located on the southern fringe of the site, behind two sweat lodges. The fill of this pit was not distinctive in any way beyond containing the two femurs. The femurs were situated such that they did not appear to be part of a disturbed or missing burial. F198 was one of the largest structures on-site, at 6.5 × 3.2 m. It was located just south of the T-shaped structure, F166, and contained rim sherds from a minimum of 53 vessels (5 Ramey Incised jars, 6 Ramey Incised sherds from other vessels, 35 other jars, 1 beaker, 2 bottles, 2 bowls, and 2 funnels). F198 fill also contained pigment, mica, and nonlocal cherts. Tools included 1 hammer, 3 abraders, 2 abraders/sanders, 3 sanders, 2 sections of chipped-stone adzes, 1 microblade core, and 2 projectile points, one a Cahokia-style and the other a Caddoan-style Hayes point (Figure 5.21).

Three more pits dating to the early to middle Stirling phase derived from isolated ceremonial events: pits F146, F209, and F287. Pit F146 occupied the southeast corner of a rebuilt meetinghouse, just north of one of the largest wall-trench buildings on-site and northeast of a large marker post. Inside it were chunks of burned thatch and mud dauber nests, as well as burned nuts, seeds, and corn. There were also 8 saws/sanders in the pit as well as 3 chunks of galena, 41 Kaolin chert flakes, and celt-making debitage. Fragments of at least 30 vessels were found as well, including 16 jars, 5 funnels, 1 jug, 1 beaker, and 6 bowls, one of which was incised.

The large wall-trench (F148) building south of F146 also seems to have received debris related to the F146 deposit. This included pigment stones, a hammerstone, a hoe fragment, an exotic Bayougoula projectile point (from Mississippi or Louisiana), a Cahokia-style projectile point, the distal end of a third chipped-stone point, fragments of an effigy vessel and 6 jars (2 of which were Ramey Incised), and celt-making debitage.

Pit F287 was located just south of house basin F148, in an area crowded with structures and rebuilt structures. It likely superimposed or was on the floor of a building that was, in turn, underneath another rebuilt structure. The pit contained heavily burned layers of thatch, fabric, corn, nuts, seeds, 1 broken celt, 1 sander/abrader, 2 hammers/grindstones, 1 spindle whorl, and portions of 15 ceramic vessels (11 jars, 1 beaker, and 3 bowls). Among the bits of burned fabric was a charred woven bag or basket with a wooden piece and cord across the top as a carry handle. Burned corn was scattered around the bag.

Similarly, F209 superimposed or was located inside a rebuilt structure (F142/F212). In it were sections of 15 vessels: 7 jars, 3 bowls, 1 seed jar, 1 jug, 1 funnel, 1 bottle, and 1 pan. As in so many of the other event deposits, there were also 4 hammers/grinders, 3 abraders, 1 grinder, pigment stones, 7 quartz crystals, and the ever-present burned thatch mixed with mud dauber nests.

Celt Cache

Less than 3 m from F209 was pit F206, a buried celt cache (Pauketat and Alt 2004). Though less than 20 cm deep, it contained 70 celts of various sizes and in various states of manufacture (Figure 5.22). The largest (46 cm long, weighing 9,145 g) was a hypertrophic specimen. It was placed as a cap for the entire cache, after which the pit was filled and sealed with sterile earth. Another celt was burned to the point of disintegration and may also have acted as a capstone of sorts.

These two and the rest were shaped from distinctive varieties of basalt and diabase originating in the St. Francois Mountains of southeast Missouri, each variety recognized through its grain size, color, and inclusions. These raw material varieties correlated to some extent with a series of dis-

Figure 5.22. Celt cache in situ, Grossmann site.

tinctive technological styles of celt, with stylistic differences evident in the manufacturing steps involving the shaping of poll or bit ends. For example, some of the celt bit ends were flared, some were squared, and others were rounded with straight sides. Stylistic choices usually clustered along with material type, seemingly signaling the choices that had been made by particular celt makers. In fact, celts made from identical raw materials and stylistic manufacturing choices were placed as sets into the pit (Pauketat and Alt 2004).

Some of the celts were unfinished, looking more like a block of stone made to resemble a celt in shape rather than an actual celt ready for use. Many of these unfinished celts had an asymmetrical appearance. The variability in how complete the manufacture of each celt was provided insight into the process of how these items were made. They were pecked and chipped into rough shape, worked from poll end to bit end, and then were sanded smooth. The last steps were the final shaping and then sharpening of the bit. Most celts were finished and might have gone into immediate use except that their bits had not received a final honing or sharpening.

Figure 5.23. Celt cache under excavation, Grossmann site, 2001.

Fourteen of those that did have sharpened bits showed macroscopic evidence of use wear.

Given the position of the pit and its lack of debris (even the flot returned clean of all but modern rootlets), it is impossible to know when in the occupation sequence the celts were deposited, and whether the celt cache and the event debris in the F209 deposit, or in the F146 deposit, were concurrent (Figure 5.23). I presume that some of the celts were made onsite, meaning that it was not a foundational deposit. But there was insufficient debitage outside the cache to account for the manufacture of 70 celts.

Human Interments

More than a cache of celts or burned figurines or heaps of Mill Creek hoe blades, abraders, crystals, and so forth were part of Grossman rituals. Mortuary events were clearly among the most important ceremonial occasions at Grossmann. The mortuary platform cannot be parsed into discrete events, but the interment of human remains can, though the chronological order of these events remains elusive. The interment of at least three sets of human remains, the burial in a courtyard, the leg bones in a pit, and the body in the bell-shaped pit of a T-shaped building were extraordinary events. Each of these three burials is an unusual, although not unique, disposition for the dead of Cahokia. The remains of 18 more individuals within the small wall-trench charnel house may have been associated with other such events.

None of these would appear to have been sacrifices similar to ridgetop mound events at Cahokia (Alt 2008; Kelly 2005; Pauketat 2010). Instead, they may have been honored or ancestral interments that celebrated or marked Grossmann as a special kind of space. This is especially true of the adult female, who had been carefully and ceremoniously wrapped and placed deep under the T building with a hint of a burned offering on her chest and the inclusion of a broken and possibly killed celt. In a certain respect, her burial is consistent with the other sorts of event-based offerings left behind at the site—from the celt cache to the repeated event-based ceremonies.

Discussion

It is important to keep in mind when considering the disposition of bodies and objects at Grossmann that people and things might all have been intimately related, with personhood itself being entangled with spirits and otherworldly powers capable of having an effect on the living both before and after sacrifice occurred (Bailey 1995; Fletcher and La Flesche 1992; Hallowell 1960; Hultkrantz 1987). Death did not always end but rather transformed an individual's interactions in the everyday world. The spirits of persons and things, living and dead, visible and invisible, would have existed in interrelated webs of relationships that would have needed to be managed and honored and kept in balance with the ancestors as well as with the living. Rituals were the ways in which relationships were and are maintained, controlled, and experienced in safety.

Given that, and the array of things engaged at Grossmann, the many deposits at that site suggest a place where ritual engagement with animate and spiritual powers was intense and ongoing (Emerson 1989, 1997b). Notably, the primary mode of engagement seems to have been through fire, as suggested by its ubiquity (on the chest of the unusually buried adult female, in the many event-based pits and basin-fill zones, as the 70th of 70 buried celts, etc.). The considerable quantity and ubiquity of woven material, broken pots, corn, tools, rare minerals, hoe blades, crystals, and other unusual items (including an archaic gorget, an ancient projectile point, and a likely bison bone fossil) suggest an unambiguous set of Cahokia-related materials if not powers present at these events. Living people were there too, of course, but it is unlikely that great communal feasts took place there, as identified at Cahokia. Certainly, the contents of the special pits do not suggest communal feasting. Nor do the recovered pots, which included various decorated containers and frequent small, individual-sized containers as much as communal-sized cook pots.

So, what were the event-based rituals? The various ingredients noted, in conjunction with human remains, hint at the kinds of "temple-based" rituals also seen in the late Stirling phase burned huts at East St. Louis (Pauketat et al. 2013). There, marking the end of the large-scale ritual-residential occupation of that precinct (and the beginning of a near-vacant Moorehead phase component), Ramey pots, bowls of corn, hoe blades, bifacial knives, and celts were piled inside 20 to several dozen buildings and then torched. The event might have been timed to the closure of a nearby ridgetop mortuary mound (Pauketat 2005). Regardless, the importance of the relationship between fire and magico-ritual materials is beyond question. At Grossmann, the near-ubiquitous presence of burned thatch and mud dauber nests in the event-based deposits suggests a similar relationship. Quite possibly, the fiery rituals were intimately linked to ceremonial renewal of the site's thatched roofs, with the high interiors of the public buildings being the most likely place for mud dauber infestations.

Put together, the evidence speaks to moments of destruction as well as moments of creation, or of death and rebirth that linked people and the spirit world. For people who see the world around them as alive with persons both human and nonhuman, objects may not be mere inanimate things, but ensouled beings or embodied animate powers or spirits. In such contexts, nothing with any ritual associations can simply be manufactured as an economic good or simply disposed of as trash. Thus, the crafting debris and killed objects were involved in a sacred cycle of life and death, similar to ethnohistorically known Green Corn or World Renewal rites (Witthoft 1949). The souls or spirits of the objects and bodies might need to be released and sent along their journey (Hall 1997; Irwin 1994). Incineration is one such means of visibly transmogrifying substance into so much smoke and fumes (Baltus and Baires 2012). Elevation of human bodies on platforms is another means, since scavenger birds (possibly depicted on one effigy bowl) would pick at the decaying flesh and fly away into the air. The burial of bones, bodies, burned ritual debris, or celts is the final means of containing the spiritual powers that remain.

6
Complexity and Hybridity Reconsidered

According to a basic dictionary definition, complexity is all about the numbers and kinds of relationships between parts. So is hybridity. We need to give much more thought to the character of both if we hope to explain the past.

The goal of this book has been to understand the causes and effects of a novel kind of American Indian phenomenon, the Mississippian world as it began at Cahokia. So far, I have done this by starting in the middle, at the intersection of Cahokia and its Richland Complex farming district. Reviewing the character of both Cahokian precincts and rural farming villages, I focused on a descriptive and qualitative analysis of the architecture and ritual remains of what may be the ideal "nodal" site (à la Emerson 1997a, 1997b). I have highlighted the general trends (Chapters 2 and 3) and laid out in detail the shape and character of the built forms and rich deposits of this ideal case (Chapters 4 and 5).

Throughout, I have emphasized that this case and other Cahokian precincts and outliers—from East St. Louis and BBB Motor to downtown Cahokia—were similar configurations of ordinary and extraordinary materials, spaces, people, and architectural constructions. In the mix, it seems to me, is the answer to the perpetual question of Cahokia's complexity. I have approached that question via a proxy question: Was there Cahokian administration of the uplands?

My answer is clearly yes, as I will explain, but it does not entail identifying the whole as this or that type of society or political economy. Instead, my answer—which admittedly remains tangled in the patterned contrasts of the archaeological data that I present in the previous chapters—recognizes that complexity always has a historical dimension. The question is not *whether* Cahokia was complex, but *how* it was complex. My answer, which is the first part of this chapter, leads me to consider the second aspect of my investigation of Cahokia's causes and effects. I seek to understand how the negotiation of administration by diverse people, places, and things generated a novel kind of early Mississippian culture. My answer to that, which is the second part of this chapter, involves extending the concepts of thirdspaces and hybridity to nonhuman objects and architectural constructions.

Did Cahokia Administer the Uplands?

On the one hand, the case for Cahokian administration of the upland farmlands of the Richland Complex seems relatively clear-cut. The chronology and characteristics of a site such as Grossmann simultaneously align with the ritual-residential remains of Cahokia even as it presents distinct contrasts with its contemporary neighbors: Halliday, Hal Smith, Knoebel, Pfeffer, and the rest. Let me review the patterns.

The first important pattern involves the history of the region. By the Edelhardt phase of the Terminal Late Woodland period (ca. A.D. 1000–1050), immediately prior to its "Big Bang" or rapid mid-eleventh-century transformation, Cahokia had grown into a large agricultural village complex. During that phase, the earliest Richland settlement at places such as Knoebel and Hal Smith was taking place. At the end of it or at the beginning of the Lohmann phase, many more farmers seem to have resettled out at the edge of the prairie east of the Mississippi floodplain. This large-scale relocation is best illustrated by the 200 or so residents of Halliday, who appeared at once on the landscape at or just before A.D. 1050. Many were immigrants, more than a third of which—judging by their pottery—came from southeast Missouri.

This occurred at the same moment, of course, as Cahokia's planned conversion into a monumental Mississippian complex. Massive construction projects, including the cutting and filling of the site's great central plaza, happened at the interface of the Terminal Late Woodland and Mississippian eras (Alt et al. 2010; Holley et al. 1993). The argument has been made that given the enormity of the labor efforts at the time, Cahokia both gave people a reason to be involved in this phenomenal transformation (Pauketat et al. 2002) and had unintended consequences (Pauketat 2000). One of the results might have been the creation of a distinctively specialized floodplain agricultural landscape, a process that Emerson (1997a, 1997b, 1997c) has previously analyzed at length. As part of this Lohmann phase ruralization, a series of farmsteads, rural nodal outlier complexes (e.g., Sponemann, Lohmann, Range), and large formal precincts (e.g., East St. Louis, St. Louis, Mitchell) replaced earlier Terminal Late Woodland villages and hamlets.

In the uplands, there was very little to replace. Instead, Lohmann phase settlement was all about emplacement. Hundreds to thousands of people must have set up residence in the hills east of the new city in fairly short order. Unlike their floodplain counterparts, they exhibited a remarkable degree of diversity. Although the sample remains modest and is only partially analyzed, each of the four sites reviewed (Halliday, Hal Smith, Knoebel, and Pfeffer) reveals similarities and dissimilarities with Lohmann phase floodplain settlements. In some ways (house forms, courtyard organization), the most unusual—possibly even "resistant"—upland settlement was Halliday (Alt 2001; Wilson 1998). In other ways (maize, shell temper), Halliday residents—owing to their origins in southeast Missouri—were more Mississippian than Cahokia.

Notably, the all-important complex at Grossmann was *not* founded in A.D. 1050. Rather, this upland diversity and all of its likely attendant implications (e.g., lack of consistent relationships with Cahokia) persisted for a generation or two until circa A.D. 1070 or 1080. Twenty to forty years had passed after the influx of relocated farmers into the uplands. By this time late in the Lohmann phase, the ritual-religious needs of farmers and the managerial sense of Cahokians might have become one and the same. After all, these villagers had arrived from diverse locations, some from Missouri (Varney culture), some from Indiana (Yankeetown culture), and others (possibly most) from elsewhere along the Mississippi or in the Illinois interior. This diversity, which may have been a driving force of Lohmann phase Cahokian change, might also have been problematic from the point of view of any centralized administration.

The site of Grossmann possessed a series of attributes that may have merged Cahokia's rituality with its administration—that distinctive mix of the ordinary and extraordinary. Unlike, say, Halliday, Hal Smith, Knoebel, and Pfeffer, it sat atop a prominent hill over 2 km from the nearest permanent water supply. From this hilltop location or nearby, residents might have surveilled the villages of Halliday, Knoebel, and many others. Other select hilltop sites might also have been visible. For instance, from the summit of the landform on which Grossmann rests, one could have seen smoke rising from Pfeffer to the northeast, Lehman-Somers to the south-southwest, and probably even the distant Miller Farm site, 9 km to the south.

Moreover, the inhabitants surrounding Grossmann could have seen it, or more precisely the rooftops of its large public structure(s) and adjacent buildings. Indeed, as one approached Grossmann, the complex of buildings around a central post must have appeared visibly distinct from any of the other settlements in the vicinity. Possibly this was a big part of what Grossmann was: it projected the appearance of Cahokia in a scaled-down form. It was a dense stand of orderly buildings and screens arranged in a horseshoe shape, a shape that identifies it even today as a "ceremonial node," similar to Sponemann (Emerson 1997a).

So too does the array of buildings at Grossmann. Unlike the single-set-post buildings of Halliday, its buildings would have had vertical walls and hipped roofs. No place in the vicinity had the complete array of what Emerson (1997a) labeled Cahokia's "architecture of power," special ritual-religious buildings that are known to have been constructed in the region *only* at some sites (such as Cahokia) and *only* between A.D. 1050 and 1200 (Emerson 2002; Pauketat et al. 2013). Yet at any given moment from the late Lohmann through middle Stirling phase, the Grossmann hilltop complex featured at least one public meetinghouse, one T-shaped building, one L-shaped building, one circular sweat lodge, and a suite of a dozen or more rectangular wall-trench structures, the last seemingly used for additional living and storage space. Off to one side for some portion of its history were both an elevated mortuary platform and an odd charnel house. Screens partitioned the open courtyard of the complex, a feature diagnostic of nodal sites in the floodplain (Emerson 1997a, 1997b; Emerson et al. 2008).

An argument that the architectural complex was visually and functionally distinct is bolstered by the materials associated with the buildings and platform, much of which can be isolated as a series of special events that took place in the screened courtyard space. Similar to Cahokia's precincts and outliers, but unlike the norm at nearby upland settlements, were distinct sets of burned construction materials (especially roof thatch), pots, clay plugs, abrading and grinding tools, hoe blades, fabric, corn, and an assortment of magico-ritual items (following Emerson 1989). The latter is characterized by a ubiquitous assemblage of quartz crystals, pigment stones, and projectile points. In addition, a limited array of craft activities was added to the mix: celt making, fiber spinning, and shell-bead making (or perforation in general). Singular artifacts stand out as well: anthropomorphic vessels, a vulture effigy bowl, a frog effigy jar, a ceramic earspool.

In some ways, Grossmann is unique even among ceremonial nodes in the greater Cahokia region. With buildings and materials spanning the religious, administrative, and civic domains, Grossmann seems reminiscent of downtown Cahokia and the East St. Louis precinct. The latter even witnessed a termination event sometime at the end of the Stirling phase, where a suite of tools, foods, and magico-ritual items that mimicked Grossmann's material assemblage was left behind in a series of storage huts to be consumed by what appears to have been a ceremonial burning of the entire complex (Pauketat et al. 2013). Of course, Grossmann had already ceased to exist by that time. The middle Stirling phase pottery and the lack of reconstruction indicate that it had been left behind a generation or two earlier.

The end of Grossmann might demarcate the beginning of the end of upland settlement. Halliday, Hal Smith, Pfeffer, Knoebel, and nearly every other settlement in the Richland Complex were all abandoned by the middle Stirling phase, if not a little earlier. There was little left of the Richland Complex after A.D. 1150, though some upland settlement east of Silver Creek is known (Holley, Parker, Harper, and Ringberg 2001; Holley, Parker, Harper, and Scott 2001; Holley, Parker, Scott, et al. 2001). Of course, during and after the Moorehead phase (A.D. 1200–1300), many people were also leaving Cahokia proper (Emerson 2002; Milner 1998; Pauketat 2004). The Grossmann experiment, perhaps, had failed.

One could presume that such a failure might have stemmed from the greater productive demands that were possibly made of the upland food producers by Cahokia through Grossmann and its nodal counterparts across the rural floodplain and upland countryside. We should not overlook the productive potential and political importance of the uplands. With perhaps 3,000 farmers around A.D. 1100, using the most conservative estimates, the Richland Complex has been likened to Cahokia's breadbasket (Benson et al. 2009; Pauketat 2003). More than this, the upland specializations—spinning in particular—would have been of great value to a burgeoning polity like Cahokia (Alt 1999). This alone suggests interdependence between villages if not also between them and downtown Cahokia.

Possibly, the most salient yet overlooked fact in support of this interdependency model is the impressive short-term aboveground storage potential of the upland sites, especially Grossmann. The paucity of storage pits and the small size of many of the buildings together form the basis of my argument that long-term domestic storage—suggestive of food stores intended for family consumption—was not the destination of most grain produced in the Richland uplands. Storage buildings are meant to be accessed during the course of a year, and Grossmann's inhabitants, with their tall buildings atop a hill overlooking the farm fields of the central portion of the Richland district, were probably doing much of the accessing.

In many ways, then, Grossmann affirms Emerson's (1997a) earlier characterization of Cahokia's relations with rural floodplain farmers. Importantly, Grossmann also holds up Emerson's sense that administration was achieved through ritual practice and religious commitment. Temples, meetinghouses, sweat lodges, and other special buildings were inhabited by people and powerful objects. The discoveries of event-related deposits at Grossmann emphasize the character and qualities of this powerful relationship. The burning and release or burial of the spiritual energies or souls of and in buildings, figurines, people, celts, and bones reveal a motivating power behind Cahokia—and a potential attraction for farmers—that is not adequately explained by considering the political economy of the Richland Complex alone.

Places such as Grossmann did much more than house specialists and appropriate the agricultural produce of the uplands. They were centers of renewal and fertility. They were places of spiritual power that mediated the worlds of the living and the dead and hence appear as simultaneously ordinary and extraordinary vis-à-vis the farming communities all around. Yes, for some Cahokians, Grossmann could have been intended to navigate and in some ways control elements of the changing social and political realities of the time. But such an intended purpose, if it existed, was seemingly never fully realized. Upland farmers adapted Cahokia for their own purposes and, ultimately, rejected it.

Extended Hybridity

The general patterns of floodplain and upland settlement before and after the founding of Grossmann allow a good argument to be made for considering two phases of the region-wide Cahokia-related process of hybridity. The first sees Cahokia and its rural floodplain nodes counterposed against an array of diverse upland sites. This initial engagement of diversity may have been a driving force of Lohmann phase Cahokian change, but that engagement happened primarily in the floodplain and at Cahokia proper. The Lohmann phase sub-Mound 51 pit at Cahokia epitomizes this phase. Beyond Cahokia across the floodplain, the initial Lohmann phase farmsteads were simpler than later Stirling phase examples (Emerson 1997a). In the uplands, the early Lohmann phase does see Cahokia-related "shrine complexes" at Pfeffer and Emerald, to the northeast, but these unusual intermittently occupied sites had widely spaced housing that did not mimic that at Cahokia (Alt and Pauketat 2017).

Grossmann epitomizes the second phase of Mississippian contact between Cahokians and the resettled farmers. We might characterize it as an overt emplacement of a piece of Cahokia in the midst of high-productivity farmlands at the height of Cahokia's development. Certainly there is overwhelming evidence of dramatic architectural and material performativity. The hilltop Grossmann complex would have projected this performative aspect outwardly with or without a farmer ever setting foot in it. However, to stop there would be to miss a significant aspect of its power as a thirdspace.

The recognition of that power begins by observing that the Grossmann site may never have been populated by a large number of people. In fact, it seems unlikely, given multiple lines of domestic-refuse and mortuary evidence, that more than a small group of elites or politico-religious specialists resided there. Perhaps only a single family and visitors ever stayed there for any significant length of time. It might even have been a facility used by Cahokians for only part of the year, with a small group of caretakers left behind in the off-seasons.

Thus, in this second phase, farmers were not necessarily coming into contact with Cahokians as much as they were Cahokian buildings and Cahokian objects, both during ritual events so clearly in evidence at Grossmann. A simple list of the raw materials and phenomenal ingredients of Grossmann rituals reveals the actors so engaged in the moments of hybridity (Table 6.1). The primary ones were fire, corn, hoe blades, mineral crystals, pigment stones (i.e., paint), thatch, mud dauber nests, fabric, and human bones (compare this list with the things imbued with power in Dorsey 1894; Hallowell 1960; Murie 1981; Radin 1990).

Of these, fire was clearly understood by many eastern Woodlands people to be related to the sun, a cosmic being that might be manifested among people by the flame (Hudson 1976). So important were the sun and fire that they were long considered by many to be the core of Mississippian religion, sometimes called the Southeastern Ceremonial Complex (Howard 1968; Snyder 1909; Squier and Davis 1848). The power of both resided in their ability *in moments* to bring about life and death, with spring and crops brought forth by sunshine and fire consuming the remains of life sent back to the earth and into the sky (Radin 1914). Fire could harden pots, cook food, warm human bodies, consume organics, and shatter stone. That is, fire transmogrified all substances, converting them from their organic or

Table 6.1. Ubiquity of Event-Deposit Materials

	Offerings/deanimations								
Event phase	Pottery	Cahokia/exotic projectile point	Fossils/ ancient artifacts	Hoe blade	Fabric	Maize	Smoking pipe	Crystal	Paint
Late Lohmann	x	x	x	x	x	x	x	x	x
Early Stirling	x	x	x	x				x	x
Other/middle Stirling	x	x	x	x	x	x		x	x

	Crafting/ritual dispensation						
Event phase	Pounding/ grinding/ sanding tools	Renewing roof thatch	Fiber spinning	Celt making	Funneling	Unplugging jugs	Drilling
Late Lohmann	x	x	x	x	x	x	x
Early Stirling	x	x	x		x		x
Other/middle Stirling	x	x	x	x	x		x

inorganic states into smoke and ash. It was an elemental kind of power (Baltus and Baires 2012).

Historically, such life-mediating power might be presenced in places and embodied through material things and living beings (Pauketat 2013b). Of course, the sun was necessary for corn to grow, and through corn, the sun was thickly entangled with earth, water, stone hoe blades, mussel-shell hoe blades, shell temper in pots, and marine-shell ornaments (Pauketat and Alt 2016). Among some likely Plains Indian descendants of Cahokia or their Mississippianized neighbors, corn was sometimes bundled with other sacred objects, the "medicine bundles" themselves being wrapped in hide and fabric (Bailey 1995; Fletcher and La Flesche 1992; Murie 1981). Other craft items, pottery-making tools, minerals, skins, arrows, smoking pipes, and parts of animals were also bundled, to be used or remembered on the occasions when those bundles were opened (Pauketat 2013b). One could easily imagine that important hoe blades might also have been held in bundles and, in turn, medicine lodges or temples. Perhaps such tools would have been the material basis for mythic stories of creation or the origins of agriculture, similar to Hargrave and Cook's (2015) understanding of a human-femur digging stick in the sub-Mound 51 feasting pit at Cahokia.

As noted, the Grossmann event deposits are filled with many of the same magico-ritual materials that showed up in both the sub-Mound 51 pit, which dates to the Lohmann phase, and the burned storage huts at East St. Louis, which date to the terminal Stirling phase (Pauketat et al. 2013; Pauketat et al. 2002). Of particular note are the mineral crystals and pigment stones. Historically, these were used in rituals by priests and shamans, and more than that, they were—like fire—opportunities for animate powers to directly engage people (Emerson 1989). Looking into a crystal was described among the Cherokee, for instance, as a transdimensional experience (Hudson 1976). Adding water to mineral pigment to make paint was described by various Siouan-speaking peoples of the Midwest and eastern plains in similar terms (Bailey 1995; Fletcher and La Flesche 1992; Radin 1990).

Given the Grossmann evidence, it seems likely that celt and bead making had a similar ritual dimension because of the exotic associations of both igneous-rock and mollusk-shell materials with distant places (Helms 1993) and because of the hints from ethnographic sources that crafting tools were part of sacred bundles (Pauketat 2013b). Certainly the presence of a cache of 70 celts at Grossmann alone suggests a special status for objects, of which at least some were probably made on-site. Given that these were laid down into the pit in sets, they may also have conveyed the relationship between the nonhuman powers of the rock with specific cultural identities of the makers of the celts. And since evidence of celt making (in the form of an unfinished celt or basalt debitage) and bead making (in the form of microlithic tool debitage) is found from at least two of the four Richland sites reviewed in Chapter 3, a number of farmers could have identified with one or another craft activity.

Fabrics and their production, along with pole-and-thatch buildings and their construction, might be even better instances of how memory-work and identity were integral parts of the process of hybridity in the second phase of upland development. Fabric is itself a kind of hybrid product, of course, consisting of organic components spun and then woven by people in ways that engender a sense of making a whole out of parts (see Chapter 1). Fabrics and spindle whorls are in ample evidence in Grossmann's event pits, and the high densities of the latter at a place such as Halliday might implicate these farmers in the creation of that whole.

Likewise, we should not overlook the builders of Grossmann's elaborate pole-and-thatch architecture or the effect of the building on the whole. That is, since Grossmann may have been inhabited by a small contingent of Cahokians or Cahokia-related representatives, it is likely that local farmers were involved in building and renewing these constructions (evident from the many deposits of burned thatch). Such laborious acts would have presumably engendered a spirit of community through the construction of collective memories and identities. In a way, the resulting buildings would have been similar to the threads in a fabric or the assemblage of celts in a cache. These were, in other words, more than a Cahokian imposition. They were hybrids, the creation of which was the process of hybridity in the uplands.

Although we lack information on the identities of the people whose bodies were exposed on the mortuary platform or whose bones were held inside the mortuary building, even the keeping of human bones at Grossmann might need to be understood in similar multidimensional hybrid terms. The bones might include the remains of a variety of people from nearby farming villages, similar to the assemblage of celts. Historically, such bones were understood to retain a soul or spiritual power, such that keeping them in a bundle, container, or building was an act that empowered the object or place (Hall 1997). But the result was not a thirdspace where living people engaged only with other living people, but rather one where the living engaged with the dead, along with a host of otherworldly powers of materials and phenomena: fire, earth, stone, crystal, corn, plant life, and more.

Conclusion

The preceding analysis of Grossmann and its place in the Cahokian sphere was conceived as an analysis of the details of the place and the events of Grossmann that would be, as far as possible, a history of a place and its people. The intent was to avoid, to in fact ignore, any categorical assignments and thus the dictates of those assignments. Indeed, we know too much about the Cahokia case to engage in such reductive explanations.

What has emerged instead is a history that elevates the middle ground, in particular the relations between people and nonhuman components, in the rise and fall of greater Cahokia. In short, I would conclude that if Cahokia was in some sense the realization of a diverse human population of locals, immigrants, and relocated farmers (which it surely was), Grossmann suggests that the central dynamic of change was not necessarily simply between people, but between people, buildings, materials, and the spiritual forces that imbued all with power. If this is true, then the history of the upland region, where both the mediating thirdspace of Grossmann and the various upland farming villages of the Richland Complex disappeared by A.D. 1150, needs to be understood as a process in which we decenter the role of people, and certainly Cahokians, as the sole agents of change. Something may have gone right and then wrong within the regional hybridity of people, places, and things that explains the beginning and the beginning of the end of Cahokia.

That is, the diversity of people, places, and things was likely important in the formation and collapse of Cahokia. Processes such as extended hybridity engendered by interactions between immigrants and Cahokians at places like Grossmann created thirdspaces that would have permitted if not spurred the cultural innovation that was behind Mississippian lifeways. Seeing change as the outgrowth of interactions between diverse actors of all sorts—including nonhuman ones—makes more sense than the old explanations that emphasize elite-centered causal scenarios. No doubt politics was still important, but the politics that mattered most might have involved power relationships between people and a much wider and hybrid field of nonhuman forces.

The data at hand are not definitive with respect to the precise causes of Cahokia's rise or fall. But I have provided some depth of field that opens up possibilities of where we should be looking for answers. That is, given the importance of fire as a principal mediating force of change, what would have been the historical effects of, say, a lightning-induced incineration of the East St. Louis complex? What if the death of a person or some other cultural event happened to coincide with a particular solar eclipse? What would have happened if the corn stopped growing as a result of droughts (Benson et al. 2009)? Would any of these nonhuman-induced perturbations have been mediated by Cahokia, via places such as Grossmann, in ways that began to unwind the fabric of the greater Cahokian phenomenon?

One might even wonder whether such unintended consequences might not have been exacerbated by the particular forms of Cahokian hybridity at any moment in time. That is, an event of the sort listed above might have had a much more profound impact in a region where the mediation of otherworldly powers was more readily accessible to or engaged in by the primary producers of some society, even if the intention had been to better administer those producers. Did Cahokia, in other words, sow the seeds of its own demise by putting pieces of itself out into the rural countryside?

Whatever events brought together Cahokians and Richland Complex farmers, it was the coming together itself, by which I mean the hybridity of living in moments and at places, that built a new polity. We need to appreciate those details. In these meetings, through manipulations of memory and ritual, and perhaps more importantly through unintended consequences of hybridity, new ways of being and new ways of understanding self and polity unfolded. Events at Grossmann celebrated the relations of the universe even as it supported a complex Cahokia polity.

The significance of the Richland Complex lies in the fact that upland farmers had an effect on, if not direct interventions in, what was happening. The earliest introduced Cahokian innovations were those that least affected the day-to-day life of farmers—changes in styles and technology but not changes in social and political organization (Alt 2001). What seems to be evident at Grossmann, however, is the increasingly intimate connections of those farmers with the fundamental powers of Cahokia. They were integrated more fully in the very essence of life, and in becoming so empowered, they may have been able to unpack the complexities of those relationships by choice or by accident.

References

Adair, James

1930 *Adair's History of the American Indians*. Promontory Press, New York.

Adovasio, James M., David C. Hyland, Olga Soffer, and Bohuslav Klimae.

2001 Perishable Industries and the Colonization of the East European Plain. In *Fleeting Identities: Perishable Material Culture in Archaeological Research*, edited by P. B. Drooker, pp. 285–313. Center for Archaeological Investigations, Occasional Paper No. 28. Southern Illinois University, Carbondale.

Ahler, Steven R., and P. J. DePuydt

1987 *A Report on the 1931 Powell Mound Excavations, Madison, County, Illinois*. Illinois State Museum, Reports of Investigations, No. 43. Springfield.

Alberti, Benjamin, Severin Fowles, Martin Holbraad, Yvonne Marshall, and Christopher Witmore

2011 "Worlds Otherwise": Archaeology, Anthropology, and Ontological Difference. *Current Anthropology* 52(6):896–912.

Alt, Susan M.

1999 Spindle Whorls and Fiber Production at Early Cahokian Settlements. *Southeastern Archaeology* 18:124–133.

2001 Cahokian Change and the Authority of Tradition. In *The Archaeology of Traditions: Agency and History before and after Columbus*, edited by T. R. Pauketat, pp. 141–156. University Press of Florida, Gainesville.

2002a Identities, Traditions, and Diversity in Cahokia's Uplands. *Midcontinental Journal of Archaeology* 27:217–236.

2002b The Knoebel Site: Tradition and Change in the Cahokian Suburbs. Master's thesis, Department of Anthropology, University of Illinois, Urbana.

2006a Cultural Pluralism and Complexity: Analyzing a Cahokian Ritual Outpost. Unpublished Ph.D. dissertation, Department of Anthropology, University of Illinois, Urbana.

2006b The Power of Diversity: The Roles of Migration and Hybridity in Culture Change. In *Leadership and Polity in Mississippian Society*, edited by

B. M. Butler and P. D. Welch, pp. 289–308. Center for Archaeological Investigations, Occasional Paper No. 33. Southern Illinois University, Carbondale.

2008 Unwilling Immigrants: Culture, Change, and the "Other" in Mississippian Societies. In *Invisible Citizens: Slavery in Ancient Pre-State Societies*, edited by C. M. Cameron, pp. 205–222. University of Utah Press, Salt Lake City.

2010 Complexity in Action(s): Retelling the Cahokia Story. In *Ancient Complexities: New Perspectives in Precolumbian North America*, edited by S. M. Alt, pp. 119–137. University of Utah Press, Salt Lake City.

2012 Making Mississippian at Cahokia. In *The Oxford Handbook of North American Archaeology*, edited by T. R. Pauketat, pp. 497–508. Oxford University Press, Oxford.

2016 Building Cahokia: Transformation through Tradition. In *Vernacular Architecture in the Pre-Columbian Americas*, edited by Christina T. Halperin and Lauren E. Schwartz, pp. 141–157. Routledge Press, New York.

Alt, Susan M. (editor)

2010 *Ancient Complexities: New Perspectives in Precolumbian North America*. University of Utah Press, Salt Lake City.

Alt, Susan M., Jeffery D. Kruchten, and Timothy R. Pauketat

2010 The Construction and Use of Cahokia's Grand Plaza. *Journal of Field Archaeology* 35(2):131–146.

Alt, Susan M., and Timothy R. Pauketat

2011 Why Wall Trenches? *Southeastern Archaeology* 30(1):108–122.

2013 *Cahokian Religion, the Emerald Pilgrimage Center, and Cultural Innovation: Preliminary Insights*. Paper presented at the RIHA Oxford Workshop, July 10, Oxford University.

2017 The Elements of Cahokian Shrine Complexes and the Basis of Mississippian Religion. In *Religion and Politics in the Ancient Americas*, edited by S. Barber and A. Joyce. University of Colorado Press, Boulder.

Anderson, David G.

1994 *The Savannah River Chiefdoms: Political Change in the Late Prehistoric Southeast*. University of Alabama Press, Tuscaloosa.

1999 Examining Chiefdoms in the Southeast: An Application of Multiscalar Analysis. In *Great Towns and Regional Polities in the Prehistoric American Southwest and Southeast*, edited by J. E. Neitzel, pp. 215–241. Amerind Foundation Publications, University of New Mexico Press, Albuquerque.

Anderson, James

1977 A Cahokia Palisade Sequence. In *Explorations into Cahokia Archaeology*, edited by M. L. Fowler, pp. 89–99. 2nd revised ed. Illinois Archaeological Survey, Bulletin No. 7. Urbana.

Appadurai, Arjun

1986 Introduction: Commodities and the Politics of Value. In *The Social Life of Things: Commodities in Cultural Perspective*, edited by A. Appadurai, pp. 3–63. Cambridge University Press, Cambridge.

1990 Disjuncture and Difference in the Global Cultural Economy. In *Global*

Culture: Nationalism, Globalization and Modernity, edited by M. Featherstone, pp. 295–310. Sage, London.

Bailey, Garrick A.

1995 *The Osage and the Invisible World from the Works of Francis La Flesche*. University of Oklahoma Press, Norman.

Baires, Sarah E.

2014 Cahokia's Origins: Religion, Complexity and Ridge-Top Mortuaries in the Mississippi River Valley. Unpublished Ph.D. dissertation, Department of Anthropology, University of Illinois, Urbana.

Baltus, Melissa R.

2014 Transforming Material Relationships: 13th Century Revitalization of Cahokian Religious-Politics. Unpublished Ph.D. dissertation, Department of Anthropology, Unviersity of Illinois, Urbana.

Baltus, Melissa R., and Sarah E. Baires

2012 Elements of Power in the Cahokian World. *Journal of Social Archaeology* 12:167–192.

Barad, Karen

2007 *Meeting the Universe Halfway: Quantum Physics and the Entanglement of Matter and Meaning*. Duke University Press, Durham, North Carolina.

Bareis, Charles J.

1976 *The Knoebel Site, St. Clair County, Illinois*. Illinois Archaeological Survey, Circular No. 1. Urbana.

Bareis, Charles J., and James W. Porter (editors)

1984 *American Bottom Archaeology: A Summary of the FAI-270 Project Contribution to the Culture History of the Mississippi River Valley*. University of Illinois Press, Urbana.

Barrier, Casey R.

2011 Storage and Relative Surplus at the Mississippian Site of Moundville. *Journal of Anthropological Archaeology* 30(2):206–219.

Basso, Keith H.

1996 *Wisdom Sits in Places: Landscape and Language among the Western Apache*. University of New Mexico Press, Albuquerque.

Beck, Robin A., Jr.

2003 Consolidation and Hierarchy: Chiefdom Variability in the Mississippian Southeast. *American Antiquity* 68:641–661.

Beehr, Dana E., and Stanley H. Ambrose

2007 Were They What They Cooked? Stable Isotopic Analysis of Mississippian Pottery Residues. In *The Archaeology of Food and Identity*, edited by K. C. Twiss, pp. 171–191. Center for Archaeological Investigations, Occasional Paper No. 34. Southern Illinois University, Carbondale.

Benchley, Elizabeth D.

1974 Mississippian Secondary Mound Loci: A Comparative Functional Analysis in a Time-Space Perspective. Unpublished Ph.D. dissertation, Department of Anthropology, University of Wisconsin, Milwaukee.

2003 Mississippian Alkali Processing of Corn. *Wisconsin Archeologist* 84:127–137.

Bennett, Jane

2010 *Vibrant Matter: A Political Ecology of Things*. Duke University Press, Durham, North Carolina.

Benson, Larry, Timothy R. Pauketat, and Edward Cook
2009 Cahokia's Boom and Bust in the Context of Climate Change. *American Antiquity* 74:467–483.
Betzenhauser, Alleen M.
2005 The Old Man Site #3 (11Ms542): A Lohmann Phase Farmstead. *Illinois Archaeology* 14:73–89.
Betzenhauser, Alleen M., Timothy R. Pauketat, Elizabeth Watts Malouchos, Neal H. Lopinot, and Daniel Marovitch
2016 The Morrison Site (11MS1548): The Case for Pre-Mississippian Mound Construction in the American Bottom. *Illinois Archaeology* 27:6–32.
Bhabha, Homi K.
1990 The Third Space. In *Identity, Community Culture, Difference*, edited by J. Rutherford, pp. 207–221. Lawrence and Wishart, London.
1994 *The Location of Culture*. Routledge, London.
Binford, Lewis R.
1962 Archaeology as Anthropology. *American Antiquity* 28:217–225.
Bird-David, Nurit
1999 "Animism" Revisited: Personhood, Environment, and Relational Epistemology. *Current Anthropology* 40(supplement):67–91.
Blasingham, Emily J.
1965 *Excavations of Yankeetown*. Report to the National Park Service, NER-815. Loyola University.
Blitz, John H.
1993 *Ancient Chiefdoms of the Tombigbee*. University of Alabama Press, Tuscaloosa.
1999 Mississippian Chiefdoms and the Fission-Fusion Process. *American Antiquity* 64:577–592.
2010 New Perspectives in Mississippian Archaeology. *Journal of Archaeological Research* 18:1–39.
Brown, Linda A., and William A. Walker
2008 Prologue: Archaeology, Animism and Non-Human Agents. *Journal of Archaeological Method and Theory* 15:297–299.
Bucko, Raymond
1998 *The Lakota Ritual of the the Sweat Lodge*. University of Nebraska Press, Lincoln.
Chapman, Robert
2003 *Archaeologies of Complexity*. Routledge, London.
Clark, John E.
2004 Mesoamerica Goes Public: Early Ceremonial Centers, Leaders, and Communities. In *Mesoamerican Archaeology: Theory and Practice*, edited by J. A. Hendon and R. A. Joyce, pp. 43–72. Blackwell, Oxford.
Clayton, Lawrence A., Vernon J. Knight Jr., and Edward C. Moore (editors)
1993 *The De Soto Chronicles: The Expedition of Hernando de Soto to North America in 1539–1543*. University of Alabama Press, Tuscaloosa.
Cobb, Charles R.
1989 An Appraisal of the Role of Mill Creek Chert Hoes in Mississippian Exchange Systems. *Southeastern Archaeology* 8:79–92.

2000 *From Quarry to Cornfield: The Political Economy of Mississippian Hoe Production*. University of Alabama Press, Tuscaloosa.
2003 Mississippian Chiefdoms: How Complex? *Annual Review of Anthropology* 32:63–84.
2005 Archaeology and the "Savage Slot": Displacement and Emplacement in the Premodern World. *American Anthropologist* 107:563–574.

Collins, James M.
1990 *The Archaeology of the Cahokia Mounds ICT-II: Site Structure*. Illinois Cultural Resources Study No. 10. Illinois Historic Preservation Agency, Springfield.
1997 Cahokia Settlement and Social Structures as Viewed from the ICT-II. In *Cahokia: Domination and Ideology in the Mississippian World*, edited by T. R. Pauketat and T. E. Emerson, pp. 124–140. University of Nebraska Press, Lincoln.

Connerton, Paul
1989 *How Societies Remember*. Cambridge University Press, Cambridge.

Crown, Patricia L., Thomas E. Emerson, J. Gu, William J. Hurst, Timothy R. Pauketat, and Timothy Ward
2012 Ritual Black Drink Consumption at Cahokia. *Proceedings of the National Academy of Sciences* 109(35):13944–13949.

Dalan, Rinita A.
1993 Landscape Modification at the Cahokia Mounds Site: Geophysical Evidence of Culture Change. Unpublished Ph.D. dissertation, Center for Ancient Studies, University of Minnesota, St. Paul.

Dalan, Rinita A., George R. Holley, William I. Woods, Harold W. Watters Jr., and John A. Koepke
2003 *Envisioning Cahokia: A Landscape Perspective*. Northern Illinois University Press, DeKalb.

Deagan, Kathleen
1996 Colonial Transformations: Euro-American Cultural Genesis in the Earliest Spanish Colonies. *Journal of Anthropological Research* 52(2):135–160.

DeBoer, Warren R.
1988 Subterranean Storage and the Organization of Surplus: The View from Eastern North America. *Southeastern Archaeology* 7(1):1–20.

Deetz, James
1996 *In Small Things Forgotten: An Archaeology of Early American Life*. Anchor Books/Doubleday, New York.

DeMott, Rodney C., Derrick J. Marcucci, and Joyce A. Williams
1993 Chipped Lithic Material. In *The Archaeology of the Cahokia Mounds ICT-II: Testing and Lithics, Part III*. Illinois Cultural Resources Study No. 9. Illinois Historic Preservation Agency, Springfield.

DePratter, Chester B.
1983 *Late Prehistoric and Early Historic Chiefdoms in the Southeastern United States*. Ph.D. dissertation, Department of Anthropology, University of Georgia, Athens. University Microfilms, Ann Arbor.

Dietler, Michael, and Brian Hayden (editors)
2001 *Feasts: Archaeological and Ethnographic Perspectives on Food, Politics, and Power*. Smithsonian Institution Press, Washington, D.C.

Dietler, Michael, and Ingrid Herbich

1998 Habitus, Techniques, Style: An Integrated Approach to the Social Understanding of Material Culture and Boundaries. In *The Archaeology of Social Boundaries*, edited by M. T. Stark, pp. 232–263. Smithsonian Institution Press, Washington, D.C.

Dincauze, Dena F., and Robert J. Hasenstab

1989 Explaining the Iroquois: Tribalization on a Prehistoric Periphery. In *Centre and Periphery: Comparative Studies in Archaeology*, edited by T. C. Champion, pp. 67–87. Unwin Hyman, London.

Dobres, Marcia-Anne

2000 *Technology and Social Agency*. Blackwell, Oxford.

Dorsey, James Owen

1894 A Study of Siouan Cults. In *Eleventh Annual Report of the Bureau of Ethnology*, pp. 351–554. Government Printing Office, Washington, D.C.

Ehrlich, Clara

1937 Tribal Culture in Crow Mythology. *Journal of American Folklore* 50(198): 307–408.

Emerson, Thomas E.

1989 Water, Serpents, and the Underworld: An Exploration into Cahokia Symbolism. In *The Southeastern Ceremonial Complex: Artifacts and Analysis*, edited by P. Galloway, pp. 45–92. University of Nebraska Press, Lincoln.

1991 Some Perspectives on Cahokia and the Northern Mississippian Expansion. In *Cahokia and the Hinterlands: Middle Mississippian Cultures of the Midwest*, edited by T. E. Emerson and R. B. Lewis, pp. 221–236. University of Illinois Press, Urbana.

1997a *Cahokia and the Archaeology of Power*. University of Alabama Press, Tuscaloosa.

1997b Cahokian Elite Ideology and the Mississippian Cosmos. In *Cahokia: Domination and Ideology in the Mississippian World*, edited by T. R. Pauketat and T. E. Emerson, pp. 190–228. University of Nebraska Press, Lincoln.

1997c Reflections from the Countryside on Cahokian Hegemony. In *Cahokia: Domination and Ideology in the Mississippian World*, edited by T. R. Pauketat and T. E. Emerson, pp. 167–189. University of Nebraska Press, Lincoln.

2002 An Introduction to Cahokia 2002: Diversity, Complexity, and History. *Midcontinental Journal of Archaeology* 27(2):127–148.

Emerson, Thomas E., Susan M. Alt, and Timothy R. Pauketat

2008 Locating American Indian Religion at Cahokia and Beyond. In *Religion, Archaeology, and the Material World*, edited by L. Fogelin, pp. 216–236. Center for Archaeological Investigations, Occasional Paper No. 36. Southern Illinois University, Carbondale.

Emerson, Thomas E., and Eve Hargrave

2000 Strangers in Paradise: Recognizing Ethnic Mortuary Diversity on the Fringes of Cahokia. *Southeastern Archaeology* 19:1–23.

Emerson, Thomas E., Eve Hargrave, and Kristin Hedman

2003 Death and Ritual in Early Rural Cahokia. In *Theory, Method, and Technique in Modern Archaeology*, edited by R. J. Jeske, pp. 163–181. Bergin and Garvey, Westport, Connecticut.

Emerson, Thomas E., and Randall E. Hughes
2000 Figurines, Flint Clay Sourcing, the Ozark Highlands, and Cahokian Acquisition. *American Antiquity* 65:79–101.
Emerson, Thomas E., and Douglas K. Jackson
1984 *The BBB Motor Site (11-Ms-595).* American Bottom Archaeology, FAI-270 Site Report No. 6. University of Illinois Press, Urbana.
Esarey, Duane, and Timothy R. Pauketat
1992 *The Lohmann Site: An Early Mississippian Center in the American Bottom.* American Bottom Archaeology, FAI-270 Site Report No. 25. University of Illinois Press, Urbana.
Evans, Madeline
2005 Lithic Remains. Report on file, Illinois State Archaeological Survey, University of Illinois Urbana-Champaign.
Faulkner, Charles H.
1977 The Winter House: An Early Southeast Tradition. *Midcontinental Journal of Archaeology* 2:141–159.
Feinman, Gary M., Kent G. Lightfoot, and Steadman Upham
2000 Political Hierarchies and Organizational Strategies in the Puebloan Southwest. *American Antiquity* 65(3):449–470.
Feinman, Gary M., and Jill E. Neitzel
1984 Too Many Types: An Overview of Sedentary Prestate Societies in the Americas. In *Advances in Archaeological Method and Theory* 7, edited by M. B. Schiffer, pp. 39–102. Academic Press, New York.
Ferguson, Leland
1992 *Uncommon Ground: Archaeology and Early African America, 1650–1800.* Smithsonian Institution Press, Washington, D.C.
Firth, Raymond
1983 *We, the Tikopia: A Sociological Study of Kinship in Primitive Polynesia.* Stanford University Press, Palo Alto, California.
Fisher, Genevieve, and Diana DiPaolo Loren
2003 Embodying Identity in Archaeology. *Cambridge Archaeological Journal* 13(2):225–230.
Flannery, Kent V.
1998 The Ground Plans of Archaic States. In *Archaic States*, edited by G. M. Feinman and J. Marcus, pp. 15–58. School of American Research Press, Santa Fe, New Mexico.
Fletcher, Alice C., and Francis La Flesche
1992 *The Omaha Tribe*, Vols. 1 and 2. Originally published 1911. University of Nebraska Press, Lincoln.
Fortier, Andrew C.
1992 Features. In *The Sponemann Site 2: The Mississippian and Oneota Occupations*, edited by D. K. Jackson, A. C. Fortier, and J. A. Williams, pp. 49–124. American Bottom Archaeology, FAI-270 Site Report No. 24. University of Illinois Press, Urbana.
1996 *The Marge Site: Late Archaic and Emergent Mississippian Occupations in the Palmer Creek Locality (11-Mo-99).* American Bottom Archaeology, FAI-270 Site Report No. 27. University of Illinois Press, Urbana.

2007 *The Archaeology of the East St. Louis Mound Center, Part II: The Northside Excavations*. Illinois Transportation Archaeological Research Program, Transportation Archaeological Research Report No. 22. University of Illinois, Urbana.

Fortier, Andrew C., and Dale L. McElrath

2002 Deconstructing the Emergent Mississippian Concept: The Case for the Terminal Late Woodland in the American Bottom. *Midcontinental Journal of Archaeology* 27:171–215.

Fowler, Melvin L.

1974 *Cahokia: Ancient Capital of the Midwest*. Addison-Wesley Module in Anthropology, No. 48. Reading, Massachusetts.

1975 A Precolumbian Urban Center on the Mississippi. *Scientific American* 233:92–101.

1978 Cahokia and the American Bottom: Settlement Archaeology. In *Mississippian Settlement Patterns*, edited by B. D. Smith, pp. 455–478. Academic Press, New York.

1997 *The Cahokia Atlas: A Historical Atlas of Cahokia Archaeology*. Illinois Transportation Archaeological Research Program, Studies in Archaeology, No. 2. University of Illinois, Urbana.

Fowler, Melvin L., Jerome C. Rose, Barbara Vander Leest, and Steven R. Ahler

1999 *The Mound 72 Area: Dedicated and Sacred Space in Early Cahokia*. Illinois State Museum, Reports of Investigations, No. 54. Springfield.

Freimuth, Glen A.

1974 The Lunsford-Pulcher Site: An Examination of Selected Traits and Their Social Implications in American Bottom Prehistory. Unpublished predissertation paper, Department of Anthropology, University of Illinois, Urbana.

Fritz, Gayle J.

1992 "Newer," "Better" Maize and the Mississippian Emergence: A Critique of Prime Mover Explanations. In *Late Prehistoric Agriculture: Observations from the Midwest*, edited by W. I. Woods, pp. 19–43. Studies in Illinois Archaeology No. 8. Illinois Historic Preservation Agency, Springfield.

Galloy, Joseph M., and Jeffery D. Kruchten

2007 *Phase II Archaeological Testing of Sites 11S9 and 11S1713, St. Clair County, Illinois*. Gateway Archaeology, St. Charles, Missouri.

Gell, Alfred

1998 *Art and Agency: An Anthropological Theory*. Oxford University Press, Oxford.

Gergen, Robert D., and William R. Iseminger

1987 *1987 Testing of Mound 50 at Cahokia Mounds State Historic Site 11-S-34*. Cahokia Mounds Museum Society, Collinsville, Illinois.

Gibbon, Guy E.

1974 A Model of Mississippian Development and Its Implications for the Red Wing Area. In *Aspects of Upper Great Lakes Anthropology*, edited by E. Johnson, pp. 129–137. Minnesota Prehistoric Archaeology Series, No. 11. St. Paul.

Giddens, Anthony
1984 *The Constitution of Society: Outline of a Theory of Structuration.* Polity Press, Cambridge.

Gilmore, Zackary I., and Jason M. O'Donaughue (editors)
2015 *The Archaeology of Events: Cultural Change and Continuity in the Pre-Columbian Southeast.* University of Alabama Press, Tuscaloosa.

Gosden, Chris
2005 What Do Objects Want? *Journal of Archaeological Method and Theory* 12(3): 193–211.

Gregg, Melissa, and Gregory J. Seigworth
2010 *The Affect Theory Reader.* Duke University Press, Durham, North Carolina.

Grinnell, George Bird
1919 A Buffalo Sweatlodge. *American Anthropologist* 21(4):361–375.

Gums, Bonnie L.
1993 Groundstone Tools, Modified Rock, and Exotic Materials. In *The Archaeology of the Cahokia Mounds ICT-II: Testing and Lithics, Part III.* Illinois Cultural Resources Study No. 9. Illinois Historic Preservation Agency, Springfield.

Halbwachs, Maurice
1992 *On Collective Memory.* Translated by L. Coser. University of Chicago Press, Chicago.

Hall, Robert L.
1991 Cahokia Identity and Interaction Models of Cahokia Mississippian. In *Cahokia and the Hinterlands: Middle Mississippian Cultures of the Midwest,* edited by T. E. Emerson and R. B. Lewis, pp. 3–34. University of Illinois Press, Urbana.
1997 *An Archaeology of the Soul: Native American Indian Belief and Ritual.* University of Illinois Press, Urbana.

Hallowell, A. I.
1960 Ojibwa Ontology, Behavior, and World View. In *Culture in History: Essays in Honor of Paul Radin,* edited by S. Diamond, pp. 19–52. Columbia University Press, New York.

Hally, David J.
1986. The Identification of Vessel Function: A Case from Northwest Georgia. *American Antiquity* 51:267–295.

Hamilakis, Yannis
2013 *Archaeology of the Senses: Human Experience, Memory, and Affect.* Cambridge University Press, Cambridge.

Hanenberger, Ned H.
2003 *The Range Site 3: Mississippian and Oneota Occupations.* Illinois Transportatation Archaeological Research Program, Research Report No. 17. University of Illinois, Urbana.

Hargrave, Eve A., and Della Cook
2015 Life after Death: A Brief History of Human Bone Tools in Submound 51 at Cahokia. In *Transforming the Dead: Culturally Modified Bone in the*

Prehistoric Midwest, edited by Eve A. Hargrave, Shirley J. Schermer, Kristin M. Hedman, and Robin M. Lillie, pp. 129–141. University of Alabama Press, Tuscaloosa.

Hargrave, Michael, David Maki, Susan M. Alt, and Timothy R. Pauketat

2002 Using Magnetic Gradiometry to Investigate an Early Mississippian Settlement. Poster presented at the Southeastern Archaeological Conference, November 7–10, Biloxi, Mississippi.

Harvey, Graham

2006 *Animism: Respecting the Living World.* Columbia University Press, New York.

Helms, Mary W.

1993 *Craft and the Kingly Ideal: Art, Trade, and Power.* University of Texas Press, Austin.

Hendon, Julia A.

2010 *Houses in a Landscape: Memory and Everyday Life in Mesoamerica.* Duke University Press, Durham, North Carolina.

Holley, George R.

1989 *The Archaeology of the Cahokia Mounds ICT-II: Ceramics.* Illinois Cultural Resources Study No. 11. Illinois Historic Preservation Agency, Springfield.

1995 Microliths and the Kunnemann Tract: An Assessment of Craft Production at the Cahokia Site. *Illinois Archaeology* 7:1–68.

Holley, George R., Rinita A. Dalan, and Phillip A. Smith

1993 Investigations in the Cahokia Site Grand Plaza. *American Antiquity* 58: 306–319.

Holley, George R., and John A. Koepke

2003 Harmony in the Cahokian World. *Wisconsin Archeologist* 84(1–2):155–164.

Holley, George R., Kathryn E. Parker, Julie H. Harper, and Jennifer E. Ringberg

2001 Mississippian Locales A–D, the J. Sprague Site (11-S-238). In *The Faust South Locality, Scott Joint-Use Archaeological Project*, edited by G. R. Holley, K. E. Parker, E. M. Scott, H. W. Watters Jr., J. H. Harper, M. Skele, A. J. Brown, D. L. Booth, J. A. Williams, and J. E. Ringberg, pp. 713–834. Vol. II. Office of Contract Archaeology, Southern Illinois University, Edwardsville.

Holley, George R., Kathryn E. Parker, Julie H. Harper, and Elizabeth M. Scott

2001 Mississippian Locales H and I, the John H. Faust Site #2 (11-S-239). In *The Faust South Locality, Scott Joint-Use Archaeological Project*, edited by G. R. Holley, K. E. Parker, E. M. Scott, H. W. Watters Jr., J. H. Harper, M. Skele, A. J. Brown, D. L. Booth, J. A. Williams, and J. E. Ringberg, pp. 977–1020. Vol. II. Office of Contract Archaeology, Southern Illinois University, Edwardsville.

Holley, George R., Kathryn E. Parker, Elizabeth M. Scott, Julie H. Harper, and Jennifer E. Ringberg

2001 Mississippian Locale E, the John H. Faust Site #1 (11-S-237). In *The Faust South Locality, Scott Joint-Use Archaeological Project*, edited by G. R. Holley, K. E. Parker, E. M. Scott, H. W. Watters Jr., J. H. Harper, M. Skele, A. J. Brown, D. L. Booth, J. A. Williams, and J. E. Ringberg, pp. 835–976.

Vol. II. Office of Contract Archaeology, Southern Illinois University, Edwardsville.

Holley, George R., Kathryn E. Parker, Harold W. Watters Jr., Julie H. Harper, Michels Skele, and Jennifer E. Ringberg

2001 *The Lembke Locality, Scott Joint-Use Archaeological Project.* Office of Contract Archaeology, Southern Illinois University, Edwardsville.

Holley, George R., Kathryn E. Parker, Harold W. Watters Jr., Julie H. Harper, Michels Skele, Jennifer E. Ringberg, Alan J. Brown, and Don L. Booth

2001 *The Knoebel Locality, Scott Joint-Use Archaeological Project.* Office of Contract Archaeology, Southern Illinois University, Edwardsville.

Howard, James H.

1968 *The Southeastern Ceremonial Complex and Its Interpretation.* Missouri Archaeological Society, Memoir No. 6. Columbia.

Howe, Jennifer

2000 Ceramic Diversity in the Uplands: American Bottom Chronology Reconsidered. *Proceedings of the 57th Annual Meeting of the Southeastern Archaeological Conference.* Macon, Georgia.

Hudson, Charles

1976 *The Southeastern Indians.* University of Tennessee Press, Knoxville.

Hultkrantz, Åke

1987 *Native Religions of North America.* Harper and Row, San Francisco.

Ingold, Tim

2000 *The Perception of the Environment: Essays in Livelihood, Dwelling and Skill.* Routledge, London.

Inomata, Takeshi, and Lawrence S. Coben (editors)

2006 *Archaeology of Performance: Theaters of Power, Community, and Politics.* AltaMira Press, Walnut Creek, California.

Irwin, Lee

1994 *The Dream Seekers: Native American Visionary Traditions of the Great Plains.* University of Oklahoma Press, Norman.

Iseminger, William R., Timothy R. Pauketat, Brad Koldehoff, Lucretia S. Kelly, and Leonard Blake

1990 *The Archaeology of the Cahokia Palisade: The East Palisade Investigations, Part I.* Illinois Cultural Resources Study No. 14. Illinois Historic Preservation Agency, Springfield.

Jackson, Douglas K.

2000 The Mississippian Community at the Grossmann Site. *Proceedings of the 57th Annual Meeting of the Southeastern Archaeological Conference.* Macon, Georgia.

2004 Ceramics from the Grossman Site, 1998 Excavations. Report on file, Illinois State Archaeological Survey, University of Illinois Urbana-Champaign.

Jackson, Douglas K., and Fred A. Finney

2007 Ceramics. In *The Archaeology of the East St. Louis Mound Center, Part II: The Northside Excavations,* edited by A. C. Fortier, pp. 663–714. Illinois Transportation Archaeological Research Program, Transportation Archaeological Research Report No. 22. University of Illinois, Urbana.

Jackson, Douglas K., Andrew C. Fortier, and Joyce A. Williams
1992 *The Sponemann Site 2 (11-Ms-517): The Mississippian and Oneota Occupations.* American Bottom Archaeology, FAI-270 Site Report No. 24. University of Illinois Press, Urbana.
Jackson, Douglas K,. and Ned H. Hanenberger
1990 *Selected Early Mississippian Household Sites in the American Bottom.* American Bottom Archaeology, FAI-270 Site Report No. 22. University of Illinois Press, Urbana.
Jackson, H. Edmund, and Susan L. Scott
1995 The Faunal Record of the Southeastern Elite: The Implications of Economy, Social Relations and Ideology. *Southeastern Archaeology* 14: 103–119.
Jones, Andrew Meirion, and Benjamin Alberti
2013 Archaeology after Interpretation. In *Archaeology after Interpretation: Returning Materials to Archaeological Theory*, edited by B. Alberti, A. M. Jones, and J. Pollard, pp. 15–35. Left Coast Press, Walnut Creek, California.
Joyce, Rosemary A.
2001 *Gender and Power in Prehispanic Mesoamerica.* University of Texas Press, Austin.
2004 Unintended Consequences? Monumentality as a Novel Experience in Formative Mesoamerica. *Journal of Archaeological Method and Theory* 11: 5–29.
Joyce, Rosemary A, and Julia A. Hendon
2000 Heterarchy, History, and Material Reality. In *The Archaeology of Communities: A New World Perspective*, edited by M. A. Canuto and J. Yaeger, pp. 143–160. Routledge, London.
Kehoe, Alice B.
1998 *Land of Prehistory: A Critical History of American Archaeology.* Routledge, London.
2002 Theaters of Power. In *The Dynamics of Power*, edited by M. O'Donovan, pp. 259–272. Center for Archaeological Investigations, Occasional Paper No. 30. Southern Illinois University, Carbondale.
2005 Wind Jewels and Paddling Gods: The Mississippian Southeast in the Postclassic Mesoamerican World. In *Gulf Coast Archaeology: The Southeastern United States and Mexico*, edited by N. M. White, pp. 260–280. University Press of Florida, Gainesville.
Kelly, John E.
1980 Formative Developments at Cahokia and the Adjacent American Bottom: A Merrell Tract Perspective. Unpublished Ph.D. dissertation, Department of Anthropology, University of Wisconsin, Madison.
1990 The Emergence of Mississippian Culture in the American Bottom Region. In *The Mississippian Emergence*, edited by B. D. Smith, pp. 113–152. Smithsonian Institution Press, Washington, D.C.
1991 The Evidence for Prehistoric Exchange and Its Implications for the Development of Cahokia. In *New Perspectives on Cahokia: Views from the Pe-*

riphery, edited by J. B. Stoltman, pp. 65–92. Prehistory Press, Madison, Wisconsin.

2005 The Archaeology of the East St. Louis Mound Center: Past and Present. In *The Archaeology of the East St. Louis Mound Center, Part I: The Southside Excavations*, edited by T. R. Pauketat, pp. 1–43. Illinois Transportation Archaeological Research Program, Transportation Archaeological Research Report No. 21. University of Illinois, Urbana.

Kelly, John E., Steven J. Ozuk, and Joyce Williams

1990 *The Range Site 2: The Emergent Mississippian Dohack and Range Phase Occupations*. American Bottom Archaeology, FAI-270 Report No. 20. University of Illinois Press, Urbana.

2007 *The Range Site 4: Emergent Mississippian George Reeves and Lindeman Phase Occupations*. Illinois Transportation Archaeological Research Program, Transportation Archaeological Research Report No. 18. University of Illinois, Urbana.

Kelly, Lucretia S.

2000 Results of Preliminary Analysis of Faunal Remains from the Halliday Site. *Proceedings of the Southeastern Archaeological Conference*. Macon, Georgia.

2001 A Case of Ritual Feasting at the Cahokia Site. In *Feasts: Archaeological and Ethnographic Perspectives on Food, Politics, and Power*, edited by M. Dietler and B. Hayden, pp. 334–367. Smithsonian Institution Press, Washington, D.C.

Kertzer, David I.

1988 *Ritual, Politics and Power*. Yale University Press, New Haven, Connecticut.

King, Adam A.

2003 *Etowah: The Political History of a Chiefdom Capital*. University of Alabama Press, Tuscaloosa.

Kinsella, Larry

2002 The Lithic Assemblage from the Lehman-Somers Site. Paper presented at the Midwestern Archaeological Conference, October 3–6, Columbus, Ohio.

Knappett, Carl

2004 The Affordances of Things: A Post-Gibsonian Perspective on the Relationality of Mind and Matter. In *Rethinking Materiality: The Engagement of Mind with the Material World*, edited by E. DeMarrais, C. Gosden, and A. C. Renfrew, pp. 43–52. MacDonald Institute for Archaeological Research, Cambridge.

Knappett, Carl, and Lambros Malafouris (editors)

2008 *Material Agency: Towards a Non-Anthropocentric Approach*. Springer, New York.

Knight, Vernon J., Jr.

1986 The Institutional Organization of Mississippian Religion. *American Antiquity* 51(4):675–687.

1989 Symbolism of Mississippian Mounds. In *Powhatan's Mantle: Indians in the Colonial Southeast*, edited by P. H. Wood, G. A. Waselkov, and M. T. Hatley, pp. 279–291. University of Nebraska Press, Lincoln.

Knight, Vernon J., and Vincas P. Steponaitis

1998 *Archaeology of the Moundville Chiefdom*. Smithsonian Institution Press, Washington, D.C.

Koldehoff, Brad

1987 The Cahokia Flake Tool Industry: Socioeconomic Implications for Late Prehistory in the Central Mississippi Valley. In *The Organization of Core Technology*, edited by J. Johnson and C. Morrow, pp. 151–186. Westview Press, Boulder, Colorado.

1995 Lithics. In *The Fingers and Curtiss Steinberg Road Sites: Two Stirling Phase Mississippian Farmsteads in the Goose Lake Locality*, edited by J. E. Kelly, pp. 41–53. Illinois Transportation Archaeological Research Program, Transportation Archaeological Research Report No. 1. University of Illinois, Urbana.

Koldehoff, Brad, Timothy R. Pauketat, and John E. Kelly

1993 The Emerald Site and the Mississippian Occupation of the Central Silver Creek Valley. *Illinois Archaeology* 5(1–2):331–343.

Kopytoff, Igor

1986 The Cultural Biography of Things: Commoditization as Process. In *The Social Life of Things: Commodities in Cultural Perspective*, edited by A. Appadurai, pp. 64–91. Cambridge University Press, Cambridge.

Kruchten, Jeffery D.

2000 Early Cahokian Fluidity on the Fringe: Pfeffer Mounds and the Richland Complex. Paper presented at the 57th Annual Southeastern Archaeological Conference, Macon, Georgia.

2012 Recent Investigations at the Knoebel Site, St. Clair County, Illinois. *Illinois Archaeology* 24.

Kruchten, Jeffery D., and Brad Koldehoff

2008 *Phase II Testing at the Stockyard Tract (11 S 706/5) for the Proposed Extension of Exchange Avenue*. Illinois Transportation Archaeological Research Program, Compliance Report No. 127. University of Illinois, Urbana.

Kus, Susan M.

1983 The Social Representation of Space: Dimensioning the Cosmological and the Quotidian. In *Archaeological Hammers and Theories*, edited by J. A. Moore and A. S. Keene, pp. 277–298. Academic Press, New York.

Kus, Susan M., and Victor Raharigaona

2000 House to Palace, Village to State: Scaling Up Architecture and Ideology. *American Anthropologist* 102(1):98–113.

Kuttruff, L. Carl

1972 *The Marty Coolidge Site, Monroe County, Illinois*. Southern Illinois Studies No. 10. University Museum, Southern Illinois University, Carbondale.

Liebmann, Matthew

2013 Parsing Hybridity: Archaeologies of Amalgamation in Seventeenth Century New Mexico. In *The Archaeology of Hybrid Material Culture*, edited by Jeb Card, pp. 25–49. Center for Archaeological Investigations, Occasional Paper No. 39. Southern Illinois University, Carbondale.

2015 The Mickey Mouse Kachina and Other "Double Objects": Hybridity in the Material Culture of Colonial Encounters. *Journal of Social Archaeology* 15:319–341.

Lightfoot, Kent G.

1995 Culture Contact Studies: Redefining the Relationship between Prehistoric and Historical Archaeology. *American Antiquity* 60:199–217.

Lightfoot, Kent G., Antoinette Martinez, and Ann M. Schiff

1998 Daily Practice and Material Culture in Pluralistic Settings: An Archaeological Study of Cultural Change and Persistence from Fort Ross, California. *American Antiquity* 63(2):199–224.

Lopatin, Ivan A.

1960 Origin of the Native American Steam Bath. *American Anthropologist* 62(6):977–993.

Loren, Diana DiPaolo

2001 Manipulating Bodies and Emerging Traditions at the Los Adaes Presidio. In *The Archaeology of Traditions*, edited by T. R. Pauketat, pp. 58–76. University Press of Florida, Gainesville.

2003 Refashioning a Body Politic in Colonial Louisiana. *Cambridge Journal of Archaeology* 13:231–237.

2007 *In Contact: Bodies and Spaces in the Sixteenth- and Seventeenth-Century Eastern Woodlands*. AltaMira Press, Lanham, Maryland.

Low, Setha M.

2000 *On the Plaza: The Politics of Public Space and Culture*. University of Texas Press, Austin.

Malinowski, Bronislaw

1961 *Argonauts of the Western Pacific*. E. P. Dutton, New York.

Marshall, Richard A.

1965 *An Archaeological Investigation of Interstate Route 55 through New Madrid and Pemiscot Counties, Missouri*. Missouri State Highway Department, Highway Archaeology Report 1.

Mauss, Marcel

1990 *The Gift: The Form and Reason for Exchange in Archaic Societies*. Translated by W. D. Halls. W. W. Norton, New York.

McGuire, Randall

1983 Breaking Down Cultural Complexity: Inequality and Heterogeneity. In *Advances in Archaeological Method and Theory 6*, edited by M. B. Schiffer, pp. 91–142. Academic Press, New York.

Mehrer, Mark W.

1995 *Cahokia's Countryside: Household Archaeology, Settlement Patterns, and Social Power*. Northern Illinois University Press, DeKalb.

Mehrer, Mark W., and James M. Collins

1995 Household Archaeology at Cahokia and in Its Hinterlands. In *Mississippian Communities and Households*, edited by J. D. Rogers and B. D. Smith, pp. 32–57. University of Alabama Press, Tuscaloosa.

Mehta, Jayur M.

2007 A Study of Sweat Lodges in the Southeastern United States. Master's thesis, Department of Anthropology, University of Alabama, Tuscaloosa.

Meskell, Lynn M.
2008 Memory Work and Material Practices. In *Memory Work: Archaeologies of Material Practices*, edited by B. J. Mills and W. H. Walker, pp. 233–243. School for Advanced Research Press, Santa Fe, New Mexico.

Meskell, Lynn M., and Rosemary A. Joyce
2003 *Embodied Lives: Figuring Ancient Maya and Egyptian Experience*. Routledge, London.

Million, Michael G.
1980 The Big Lake Phase Pottery Industry. In *Zebree Archeological Project: Excavation, Data Interpretation, and Report on the Zebree Homestead Site, Mississippi County, Arkansas*, edited by D. F. Morse and P. A. Morse, pp. 1–42. Memphis District, U.S. Army Corps of Engineers, Contract No. DACW66-76-C-0006. Memphis, Tennessee.

Mills, Barbara J.
2004 The Establishment and Defeat of Hierarchy: Inalienable Possessions and the History of Collective Prestige Structures in the Pueblo Southwest. *American Anthropologist* 106(2):238–251.

Mills, Barbara J., and William H. Walker
2008 Memory, Materiality, and Depositional Practice. In *Memory Work: Archaeologies of Material Practices*, edited by B. J. Mills and W. H. Walker, pp. 3–24. School for Advanced Research Press, Santa Fe, New Mexico.

Mills, Barbara J., and William H. Walker (editors)
2008 *Memory Work: Archaeologies of Material Practices*. School for Advanced Research Press, Santa Fe, New Mexico.

Milner, George R.
1984a *The Robinson's Lake Site*. American Bottom Archaeology, FAI-270 Site Report No. 10. University of Illinois Press, Urbana.
1984b Social and Temporal Implications of Variation among American Bottom Mississippian Cemeteries. *American Antiquity* 49:468–488.
1998 *The Cahokia Chiefdom: The Archaeology of a Mississippian Society*. Smithsonian Institution Press, Washington, D.C.

Milner, George R., Thomas E. Emerson, Mark W. Mehrer, Joyce Williams, and Duane Esarey
1984 Mississippian and Oneota Period. In *American Bottom Archaeology*, edited by C. J. Bareis and J. W. Porter, pp. 158–186. University of Illinois Press, Urbana.

Minar, Jill
2001 Material Culture and the Identification of Prehistoric Cultural Groups. In *Fleeting Identities: Perishable Material Culture in Archaeological Research*, edited by P. B. Drooker, pp. 94–113. Center for Archaeological Investigations, Occasional Paper No. 28. Southern Illinois University, Carbondale.

Moorehead, Warren K.
2000 *The Cahokia Mounds*. University of Alabama Press, Tuscaloosa.

Morse, Dan F., and Phyllis A. Morse
1983 *Archaeology of the Central Mississippi Valley*. Academic Press, New York.

Muller, Jon D.
1986 *Archaeology of the Lower Ohio River Valley*. Academic Press, New York.
1997 *Mississippian Political Economy*. Plenum Press, New York.
Murie, James R.
1981 *Ceremonies of the Pawnee, Part I: The Skiri*. Smithsonian Contributions to Anthropology, No. 27. Smithsonian Institution Press, Washington, D.C.
Neitzel, Jill
1999 Examining Societal Organization in the Southwest: An Application of Multiscalar Analysis. In *Great Towns and Regional Polities in the Prehistoric American Southwest and Southeast*, edited by J. Neitzel, pp. 183–214. Amerind Foundation Publications, University of New Mexico Press, Albuquerque.
Nelson, Ben A.
1995 Complexity, Hierarchy and Scale: A Controlled Comparison between Chaco Canyon, New Mexico, and La Quemada, Zacatecas. *American Antiquity* 60:597–618.
O'Brien, Michael J.
2001 *Mississippian Community Organization: The Powers Phase in Southeastern Missouri*. Kluwer Academic/Plenum Publishers, New York.
O'Brien, Patricia J.
1969 The Chronological Position of the Cambered Jar at Cahokia and Its Implications. *American Antiquity* 34(4):411–416.
1989 Cahokia: Political Capital of the "Ramey" State? *North American Archaeologist* 10:275–292.
Otten, Sarah E.
2011 Pieces of Personhood: Religious Spaces, Ritual Practices, and Human Remains at Three Upland Mississippian Sites in the American Bottom. Unpublished Master's thesis, Department of Anthropology, University of Illinois, Urbana.
Otten, Sarah E., Melissa R. Baltus, and Timothy R. Pauketat
2007 Prayers on Cahokia's Periphery: New Evidence of Temple Ritual and Earthen Symbolism at the Pfeffer Site. Paper presented at the 64th Southeastern Archaeological Conference, Knoxville, Tennessee.
Pauketat, Timothy R.
1993 *Temples for Cahokia Lords: Preston Holder's 1955–1956 Excavations of Kunnemann Mound*. Memoirs of the University of Michigan Museum of Anthropology, No. 26. University of Michigan, Ann Arbor.
1994 *The Ascent of Chiefs: Cahokia and Mississippian Politics in Native North America*. University of Alabama Press, Tuscaloosa.
1997 Cahokian Political Economy. In *Cahokia: Domination and Ideology in the Mississippian World*, edited by T. R. Pauketat and T. E. Emerson, pp. 30–51. University of Nebraska Press, Lincoln.
1998a *The Archaeology of Downtown Cahokia: The Tract 15A and Dunham Tract Excavations*. Illinois Transportation Archaeological Research Program, Studies in Archaeology, No. 1. University of Illinois, Urbana.
1998b Refiguring the Archaeology of Greater Cahokia. *Journal of Archaeological Research* 6:45–89.

2000 The Tragedy of the Commoners. In *Agency in Archaeology*, edited by M.-A. Dobres and J. Robb, pp. 113–129. Routlege, London.

2001 Practice and History in Archaeology: An Emerging Paradigm. *Anthropological Theory* 1:73–98.

2003 Resettled Farmers and the Making of a Mississippian Polity. *American Antiquity* 68:39–66.

2004 Archaeology without Alternatives. *Anthropological Theory* 4:199–203.

2005 Mounds, Buildings, Posts, Palisades, and Compounds. In *The Archaeology of the East St. Louis Mound Center, Part I: The Southside Excavations*, edited by T. R. Pauketat, pp. 113–192. Illinois Transportation Archaeological Research Program, Transportation Archaeological Research Report No. 21. University of Illinois, Urbana.

2007 *Chiefdoms and Other Archaeological Delusions*. AltaMira Press, Walnut Creek, California.

2010 The Missing Persons in Mississippian Mortuaries. In *Mississippian Mortuary Practices: Beyond Hierarchy and the Representationist Perspective*, edited by L. P. Sullivan and R. C. Mainfort, pp. 14–29. University Press of Florida, Gainesville.

2013a *The Archaeology of Downtown Cahokia II: The 1960 Excavation of Tract 15B*. Studies in Illinois Archaeology 8. Illinois State Archaeological Survey, Urbana.

2013b *An Archaeology of the Cosmos: Rethinking Agency and Religion in Ancient America*. Routledge, London.

Pauketat, Timothy R. (editor)

2005 *The Archaeology of the East St. Louis Mound Center, Part I: The Southside Excavations*. Illinois Transportation Archaeological Research Program, Transportation Archaeological Research Report No. 21. University of Illinois, Urbana.

Pauketat, Timothy R., and Susan M. Alt

2004 The Making and Meaning of a Mississippian Axe-Head Cache. *Antiquity* 78:779–797.

2015 *Medieval Mississippians: The Cahokian World*. School for Advanced Research Press, Santa Fe, New Mexico.

2016 Water and Shells in Bodies and Pots: Mississippian Rhizome, Cahokian Poiesis. In *Relational Identities and Other-Than-Human Agency in Archaeology*, edited by E. Harrison-Buck and J. Hendon. University of Colorado Press, Boulder.

Pauketat, Timothy R., Susan M. Alt, and Jeffery D. Kruchten

2015 City of Earth and Wood: Cahokia and Its Material-Historical Implications. In *A World of Cities*, edited by N. Yoffee, pp. 437–454. Cambridge University Press, Cambridge.

2017 The Emerald Acropolis: Elevating the Moon and Water in the Rise of Cahokia. *Antiquity* 91(355):207–222.

Pauketat, Timothy R., Susan M. Alt, and Janet M. Pauketat

2005 Some Problems Detecting Mississippian Farmsteads in Southwestern Illinois. *Illinois Archaeology* 17:154–167.

Pauketat, Timothy R., and Thomas E. Emerson
1991 The Ideology of Authority and the Power of the Pot. *American Anthropologist* 93(4):919–941.
1997 Introduction: Domination and Ideology in the Mississippian World. In *Cahokia: Domination and Ideology in the Mississippian World*, edited by T. R. Pauketat and T. E. Emerson, pp. 30–51. University of Nebraska Press, Lincoln.
1999 The Representation of Hegemony as Community at Cahokia. In *Material Symbols: Culture and Economy in Prehistory*, edited by J. E. Robb, pp. 302–317. Center for Archaeological Investigations, Occasional Paper No. 26. Southern Illinois University, Carbondale.

Pauketat, Timothy R., and Thomas E. Emerson (editors)
1997 *Cahokia: Domination and Ideology in the Mississippian World*. University of Nebraska Press, Lincoln.

Pauketat, Timothy R., Andrew C. Fortier, Thomas E. Emerson, and Susan M. Alt
2013 A Mississippian Conflagration and Its Historical Implications. *Journal of Field Archaeology* 38:208–224.

Pauketat, Timothy R., Lucretia S. Kelly, Gayle J. Fritz, Neal H. Lopinot, Scott Elias, and Eve Hargrave
2002 The Residues of Feasting and Public Ritual at Early Cahokia. *American Antiquity* 67:257–279.

Pauketat, Timothy R., Jeffery D. Kruchten, and Susan M. Alt
2002 *Phase II Cultural Resource Evaluation and Testing of the TRDS Property, Shiloh, Illinois*. Report submitted to the Illinois Historic Preservation Agency, Springfield.

Pauketat, Timothy R., Jeffery D. Kruchten, Melissa R. Baltus, Kathryn E. Parker, and Elizabeth Kassly
2012 An Ancient Medicine Lodge in the Richland Complex. *Illinois Archaeology* 24:159–183.

Pauketat, Timothy R., and Neal H. Lopinot
1997 Cahokian Population Dynamics. In *Cahokia: Domination and Ideology in the Mississippian World*, edited by T. R. Pauketat and T. E. Emerson, pp. 103–123. University of Nebraska Press, Lincoln.

Pauketat, Timothy R., Mark A. Rees, and Stephanie L. Pauketat
1998 *An Archaeological Survey of Horseshoe Lake State Park, Madison County, Illinois*. Illinois State Museum, Report of Investigations, No. 55. Springfield.

Payne, Claudine
1994 Mississippian Capitals: An Archaeological Investigation of Precolumbian Political Structure. Unpublished Ph.D. dissertation, Department of Anthropology, University of Florida, Gainesville.

Peregrine, Peter
1992 *Mississippian Evolution: A World System Perspective*. Monographs in World Archaeology No. 9. Prehistory Press, Madison.

Perino, Gregory
1971 The Mississippian Component at the Schild Site No. 4, Greene County,

Illinois. In *Mississippian Site Archaeology in Illinois: 1*, pp. 1–148. Illinois Archaeological Survey, Bulletin No. 8. Urbana.

Phillips, Philip, and James A. Brown
1978 *Pre-Columbian Shell Engravings from the Craig Mound at Spiro, Oklahoma.* Peabody Museum of Archaeology and Ethnology, Harvard University, Cambridge, Massachusetts.

Porter, James W.
1969 The Mitchell Site and Prehistoric Exchange Systems at Cahokia: A.D. 100 + 300. In *Explorations into Cahokia Archaeology*, edited by M. L. Fowler, pp. 137–164. Illinois Archaeological Survey, Bulletin No. 7. Urbana.
1974 *Cahokia Archaeology as Viewed from the Mitchell Site: A Satellite Community at A.D. 1150–1200.* Ph.D. dissertation, Department of Anthropology, University of Wisconsin, Madison.
1984 Thin Section Analysis of Ceramics. In *The Robinson's Lake Site (11-Ms-582)*, edited by G. R. Milner, pp. 133–216. American Bottom Archaeology, FAI-270 Site Report No. 10. Urbana.

Possehl, Gregory L.
1997 The Transformation of the Indus Civilization. *Journal of World Prehistory* 11(4):425–472.

Radin, Paul
1914 Religion of the North American Indians. *Journal of American Folklore* 27:335–373.
1990 *The Winnebago Tribe.* University of Nebraska Press, Lincoln. Originally published 1923.

Rapoport, Amos
1982 Sacred Places, Sacred Occasions and Sacred Environments. *Architectural Design* 52(9–10):75–82.
1990 *The Meaning of the Built Environment: A Nonverbal Communication Approach.* University of Arizona Press, Tucson.

Reber, Eleanora A., and Richard P. Evershed
2006 Ancient Vegetarians? Absorbed Pottery Residue Analysis of Diet in the Late Woodland and Emergent Mississippian Periods of the Mississippi Valley. *Southeastern Archaeology* 25(1):111–120.

Rose, Jerome C.
1999 Mortuary Data and Analysis. In *The Mound 72 Area: Dedicated and Sacred Space in Early Cahokia*, edited by M. L. Fowler, J. C. Rose, B. Vander Leest, and S. R. Ahler, pp. 63–82. Illinois State Museum, Reports of Investigations, No. 54. Springfield.

Rowlands, M. J.
1993 The Role of Memory in the Transmission of Culture. *World Archaeology* 25(2):141–151.

Scarry, John F.
1996 *Political Structure and Change in the Prehistoric Southeastern United States.* University Press of Florida, Gainesville.

Schroeder, Sissel
2004 Power and Place: Agency, Ecology, and History in the American Bottom, Illinois. *Antiquity* 78:812–827.

Sherwood, Sarah C., and Tristram R. Kidder
2011 The DaVincis of Dirt: Geoarchaeological Perspectives on Native American Mound Building in the Mississippi River Basin. *Journal of Anthropological Archaeology* 30:69–87.

Sillar, Bill
2009 The Social Agency of Things? Animism and Materiality in the Andes. *Cambridge Archaeological Journal* 19(3):367–377.

Silliman, Stephen W.
2005 Culture Contact or Colonialism? Challenges in the Archaeology of Native North America. *American Antiquity* 70(1):55–74.
2013 What, Where, and When Is Hybridity? In *The Archaeology of Hybrid Material Culture*, edited by Jeb Card, pp. 486–500. Center for Archaeological Investigations, Occasional Paper No. 39. Southern Illinois University, Carbondale.
2015 A Requiem for Hybridity? The Problem with Frankensteins, Purées, and Mules. *Journal of Social Archaeology* 15(3):277–298.

Simon, Mary L., and Kathryn E. Parker
2006 Prehistoric Plant Use in the American Bottom: New Thoughts and Interpretations. *Southeastern Archaeology* 25(2):212–257.

Slater, Philip A., Kristin M. Hedman, and Thomas E. Emerson
2014 Immigrants at the Mississippian Polity of Cahokia: Strontium Isotope Evidence for Population Movement. *Journal of Archaeological Science* 44: 117–127.

Smith, Bruce D.
1978 Variation in Mississippian Settlement Patterns. In *Mississippian Settlement Patterns*, edited by B. D. Smith, pp. 479–503. Academic Press, New York.

Smith, Harriet
1969 The Murdock Mound, Cahokia Site. In *Explorations into Cahokia Archaeology*, edited by M. L. Fowler, pp. 49–88. Illinois Archaeological Survey, Bulletin No. 7. Urbana.

Snyder, John Francis
1909 Prehistoric Illinois, Certain Indian Mounds Technically Considered, Part Second: Sepulchral and Memorial Mounds. *Journal of the Illinois State Historical Society* 2(1):47–65.

Soja, Edward W.
1996 *Thirdspace*. Blackwell, Oxford.

Spielmann, Katherine A.
2002 Feasting, Craft Specialization, and the Ritual Mode of Production in Small-Scale Societies. *American Anthropologist* 104(1):195–207.

Squier, Ephraim G., and Edwin G. Davis
1848 *Ancient Monuments of the Mississippi Valley*. Smithsonian Institution Contributions to Knowledge, Vol. 1. Washington, D.C.

Steponaitis, Vincas P.
1983 *Ceramics, Chronology, and Community Patterns: An Archaeological Study at Moundville*. Academic Press, New York.
1991 Contrasting Patterns of Mississippian Development. In *Chiefdoms: Power,*

Economy, and Ideology, edited by Timothy K. Earle, pp. 193–228. Cambridge University Press, New York.

Steponaitis, Vincas P., and C. Margaret Scarry (editors)
2016 *Rethinking Moundville and Its Hinterland*. University Press of Florida, Gainesville.

Stewart, Kathleen
2007 *Ordinary Affects*. Duke University Press, Durham, North Carolina.

Sullivan, Lynne P., and Christopher B. Rodning
2001 Gender, Tradition, and the Negotiation of Power Relationships in Southern Appalachian Chiefdoms. In *The Archaeology of Traditions: Agency and History before and after Columbus*, edited by T. R. Pauketat, pp. 107–120. University Press of Florida, Gainesville.

Swanton, John R.
1979 *The Indians of the Southeastern United States*. Smithsonian Institution Press, Washington, D.C.

Sztompka, P.
1991 *Society in Action: The Theory of Social Becoming*. University of Chicago Press, Chicago.

Tarlow, Sarah
2012 The Archaeology of Emotion and Affect. *Annual Review of Anthropology* 41:169–185.

Trubitt, Mary Beth D.
2000 Mound Building and Prestige Goods Exchange: Changing Strategies in the Cahokia Chiefdom. *American Antiquity* 65:669–690.

Turner, Victor
1974 *Dramas, Fields, and Metaphors: Symbolic Action in Human Society*. Cornell University Press, Ithaca, New York.

van Dommelen, Peter
1997 Colonial Constructs: Colonialism and Archaeology in the Mediterranean. *World Archaeology* 28(3):305–323.

Van Dyke, Ruth M., and Susan E. Alcock (editors)
2003 *Archaeologies of Memory*. Blackwell, Oxford.

Vogel, Joseph O.
1975 Trends in Cahokia Ceramics: Preliminary Study of the Collections from Tracts 15A and 15B. In *Perspectives in Cahokia Archaeology*, edited by M. Fowler, pp. 32–125. Illinois Archaeological Survey, Bulletin No. 10. Urbana.

Walker, William H.
2008 Practice and Nonhuman Social Actors: The Afterlife Histories of Witches and Dogs in the American Southwest. In *Memory Work: Archaeologies of Material Practices*, edited by B. J. Mills and W. H. Walker, pp. 137–158. School for Advanced Research Press, Santa Fe, New Mexico.

Waselkov, Gregory A., and Kathyrn E. Holland Braund (editors)
1995 *William Bartram on the Southeastern Indians*. University of Nebraska Press, Lincoln.

Weiner, Annette
1992 *Inalienable Possessions: The Paradox of Keeping-While-Giving*. University of California Press, Berkeley.

Weismantel, Mary, and Lynn Meskell
2014 Substances: "Following the Material" through Two Prehistoric Cases. *Journal of Material Culture* 19(3):233–251.
Welch, Paul D.
1991 *Moundville's Economy*. University of Alabama Press, Tuscaloosa.
Welch, Paul D., and C. Margaret Scarry
1995 Status-Related Variation in Foodways in the Moundville Chiefdom. *American Antiquity* 60(3):397–419.
Wesselmann, Jill
2000 The Politics of Family: Implications of Courtyard Construction and Group Movement in the Uplands. Paper presented at the 57th Annual Southeastern Archaeological Conference, Macon, Georgia.
Williams, Joyce
1992 Lithics. In *The Sponemann Site 2: The Mississippian and Oneota Occupations*, edited by D. K. Jackson, A. C. Fortier, and J. A. Williams. American Bottom Archaeology, FAI-270 Report No. 24. University of Illinois Press, Urbana.
Williams, Stephen
1954 An Archaeological Study of the Mississippian Culture in Southeast Missouri. Unpublished Ph.D. dissertation, Department of Anthropology, Yale University, New Haven, Connecticut.
Wilson, Gregory D.
1998 A Case Study of Mississippian Resistance in the American Bottom. Unpublished Master's thesis, Department of Anthropology, University of Oklahoma, Norman.
Witmore, Christopher
2014 Archaeology and the New Materialisms. *Journal of Contemporary Archaeology* 1(2):203–246.
Witthoft, John
1949 *Green Corn Ceremonialism in the Eastern Woodlands*. University of Michigan, Museum of Anthropology, Occasional Contributions 13. Ann Arbor.
Wittry, Warren L.
1964 An American Woodhenge. *Cranbrook Institution of Science News Letter* 33(9):49–55.
Wittry, Warren L., John C. Arnold, Charles O. Witty, and Timothy R. Pauketat
1994 *The Holdener Site: Late Woodland, Emergent Mississippian, and Mississippian Occupations in the American Bottom Uplands*. American Bottom Archaeology, FAI-270 Site Report No. 6. University of Illinois Press, Urbana.
Yerkes, Richard W.
1983 Microwear, Microdrills, and Mississippian Craft Specialization. *American Antiquity* 48:499–518.
Yoffee, Norman
1993 Too Many Chiefs? (or, Safe Texts for the '90s). In *Archaeological Theory: Who Sets the Agenda*, edited by N. Yoffee and A. Sherratt, pp. 60–78. Cambridge University Press, Cambridge.
2005 *Myths of the Archaic State: Evolution of the Earliest Cities, States and Civilization*. Cambridge University Press, Cambridge.

Yoffee, Norman, Suzanne K. Fish, and George R. Milner
1999 Comunidades, Ritualities, Chiefdoms: Social Evolution in the American Southwest and Southeast. In *Great Towns and Regional Polities in the Prehistoric American Southwest and Southeast*, edited by J. E. Neitzel, pp. 261–271. University of New Mexico Press, Albuquerque.

Young, Bilone W., and Melvin L. Fowler
2000 *Cahokia: The Great Native American Metropolis*. University of Illinois Press, Urbana.

Index